ONE MAN'S ONE WORLD

ONE MAN'S ONE WORLD

Buck Scott

Copyright © 2004 by Buck Scott.

Library of Congress Number: 2004094357
ISBN : Hardcover   1-4134-6090-9
        Softcover   1-4134-6089-5

All rights reserved. No part of this book may be reproduced or transmitted in any form or by any means, electronic or mechanical, including photocopying, recording, or by any information storage and retrieval system, without permission in writing from the copyright owner.

This book was printed in the United States of America.

To order additional copies of this book, contact:
Xlibris Corporation
1-888-795-4274
www.Xlibris.com
Orders@Xlibris.com
25792

CONTENTS

Why?	7
Technology	12
Leisure	25
Organization	42
Ideology	59
Gender, Race & Class	72
Celebrities	81
Expatriation	87
Communication	94
Finance	108
Health & Education	119
Strategy	127
Forward Thoughts	135

WHY?

Sometime between the shyness of boyhood and the zeal of young manhood I started to become a citizen of the world. Radios continuously brought me the horrors of the Spanish Civil War and then of the Nazis. I watched the American people first reject, and then plunge into an international war. I visited my mother's Canada, and realized there was a difference between the U.S. and other nations. Two English refugee children joined our family for five years of the War. In our family, we grew up with the idea of global involvement.

It was a natural evolution for me, and by the time I was 20 and in College, I had long-since adopted a favorable attitude toward humanity at large. It seemed that the United States was not only the victor in a mammoth war, but the leader in a world peace. In the name of global stability and under the titular banner of the United Nations, I went to the Korean War. This was an action which was disturbing to my life plans as they then were, but I justified it in my mind as a contribution to a rapidly evolving world system. In later years of greater sophistication, I endorsed many globalizing trends, and watched with satisfaction the world's progress, which was more profound than I would have thought possible half a century ago. I tried to contribute to efforts of peace and good will in the fields I touched, and now the time has come to review the remarkable factors which have changed our world

For all of that, the career of being a citizen of the world, and a participant in the system that goes with it, is not complete. I am less worried that we will commit world suicide than I was 50 years ago, but even so, there are dangers. I am not ready to relax and rely on the inevitability of world peace and stability.

I offer detail about my own opinions and experience to show how one person's mind evolved quite smoothly into a general internationalist position. Possibly I am one of a kind, but I think not. My findings are not unique, my opinions neither radical nor original, and this is not an autobiography. I select particular episodes and assert personal conclusions, hoping that you, the reader, will recognize a thread of analysis which has come from one man's life, but it could be yours.

I draw on some facts and introspection about myself in getting to the larger question of how and why the world is making such progress in organizing itself. Just as a scientist does experiments and records data to establish a base position from which later changes can be observed, I relate circumstances during my lifetime. They have a measurable effect on the global situation.

Of course, the world has *always* been global, but present times offer novel changes and possibilities, some of which I relate. We like to think that individual thought and action is necessary to move anything forward, and even the writing of this book is one man's presentation of that human need. However, I maintain that most of what is happening now in the world is the result of broad trends in society which sweep through even the sleepiest backwaters. I will leave to others the determination of just which individual actions initiate these trends.

A yearning for organization has arisen in the past several hundred years. The world's peoples, unevenly but steadily, have emerged from tribalism, feudalism and hereditary structures. There have been universal attempts to regularize and codify human governing arrangements, and this is best demonstrated by the present maintenance of 191 nation states. It seems that these have been around forever, but of course they have not. The kingdom of Great Britain, for example, came into existence only with the Act of Union between England and Scotland in 1704.

Many of today's nations are creations of the 20th century. Iraq, Israel, South Korea, Egypt are four that come to mind. And there are many others that grew out of recent colonialism, ancient empires that changed into nations, or other constructions. At first glance these 191 appear to be competitors, but a closer look reveals that they deeply need to cooperate with each other, and that this cooperation, alliance building, and networking is the main trend of the current day. It has taken several hundred years for the world's citizens even to get comfortable with the idea of nations. Now, however, the dynamics of history are demanding that this comfort be raised to an international level.

The United States is the de facto headquarters of a world empire. That empire is a new creation, transcending existing boundaries. It is certainly possible that some other group . . . perhaps the Chinese . . . could come to dominate that empire in future, but for the moment, U.S. needs, aspirations and capabilities dominate the governance of the world. The U.S. supplies about 1/3 of the world's gross economic output, with Europe supplying another third, and the balance by all the rest. Many smaller nations rely on transactions with the bigger economic groups to provide a living for their populations. Much of this reliance centers on exports of commodities ranging from coffee beans to copper to fertilizer to oil. And the big developed countries have significant export markets for their machinery and services. The commercial interests who control these markets make it plain to governments that their profit plans, and therefore the revenue of the governments, depends ever more on the flow of money connected with this activity, roughly called "trade".

This is not to say that economics rules everything. Famous one-liners like "It's the economy, stupid" or "The business of America is business" are exaggerations. U.S. influence in the arts, religion and science is powerful. Many matters are benchmarked, negatively or positively, in relationship to U.S. standards. The future for these matters may be different, but at this time the U.S. has a disproportionate influence in conceptual as well as in hard commercial matters.

Leaders of governments are quoted in headlines declaring their patriotic demands and intentions for their nations. But behind the scenes, sober considerations prevail, and this drives more and more nations to restrain their extreme wish-lists, and instead seek cooperation with potential and existing client states. International organizations are, year after year, racking up new and detailed cooperative arrangements which have the declared or unspoken approval of an increasing number of regimes. The oil cartel, once a feared and mis-understood group, has gone main-stream, for example. Its regular Vienna meetings, where production goals and prices are periodically announced, get attention from all. The important suppliers of oil outside the cartel speak respectfully of its decisions, and in fact count on those decisions to define their own possibilities.

Meanwhile, the World Trade Organization has begun to systematize the terms of trade, most notably recently for China. The arrangements for legal and accounting treatment of business activities across national boundaries are increasingly subject to international negotiation and restraint. The actions of most large international businesses are scrutinized not only by the free-falling, free-rising tendencies of the marketplace, but more and more are involved with agreed-upon rules, international approvals, and contracts which involve many international parties.

There is frustration and rebellion on the part of many organizations which get caught up in this web of other people looking over many shoulders. For example, the European Union's officials have started scrutinizing business combinations and mergers more and more with respect to "anti-trust" considerations. And who taught those Europeans to inaugurate such a refined economic concept? The Americans, prodded originally by President Theodore Roosevelt. In a world which has, since the dawn of history, had trade restraint and control as a major feature of society, it is objectionable to be told that *your* business deal and *your* perpetual exclusive franchise to make money is subject to the invisible hand of competition, and world-wide competition at that. For many people, it is a very new and hard doctrine. Yet the demand for international competition in a million different matters is growing exponentially, irrespective of the wishes of traditional governments, companies, labor unions, and other interested parties.

We are now privileged to observe, through statistics, polls, and fast communication, thousands of activities which it was difficult or impossible to know of 100 years ago. Instantaneous evaluation of this information is a major business, whether it is in the field of advertising and public relations, marketing, selling or banking. The world's economic and social welfare is subject to this milieu. The number of active participants sharing the immense amount of data is beyond the control of the current structures; those participants will ultimately re-shape the world's organizations to meet the needs of society. Also it may be hoped that superfluous organizations will wither along the way.

Despite positive moves either compelled by natural forces or extracted through reasoned leadership, the world is still in organizational flux. Narrowly-specialized experts and technicians, particularly in the fields of politics, commerce, and religion, can and do advocate separatist unilateral actions opposed to the common interests of humanity, and they can be extremely persuasive and influential. Opportunities for social disintegration exist at both national and international levels, but I believe that the *need* for sensible world arrangements will drive matters more than mere hope for them.

Optimism is the state of mind I find most congenial in myself and others. However, despite this outlook I try to maintain a level of skepticism about the world as I see it. I do not utterly approve of the ideas and actions of any single nation or group in the world. I also respect those who take the trouble to question my views. I would be disappointed if they did not. I also admire the work of critics who work in the public domain, and especially those who think, print and say unpopular thoughts. My own position is that of a 75-year old male Pennsylvania native, living here as a world citizen in 2004, and from that viewpoint I offer more details about the world as I have come to know it.

TECHNOLOGY

Technology is a headline word for things that are small, like micro-chips, or complicated, like communication systems. It's an old word, and it was a favorite as a name choice for institutions of higher learning established in the 19th century. In the public mind, technology was machines made of metal, with wondrous functioning interrelationships. No wonder the Drexel Institute of Technology or California Institute of Technology adopted such a description of themselves. It was all the rage, though new aspirations have now led to the adoption of the name "university" to cover all bases, and "Institute" is old-fashioned.

Technology, whether it is practiced in design and making of farm machinery, chemical products, in mineral extraction or astrophysical explorations, is now the leading factor in world life, but its development has been uneven in geographical terms. The United States is still a major technological leader, although many other nations are sources of fine science, which you can verify by consulting the pages of learned journals to see who is writing papers. Because we cannot know the origins of good ideas until they occur, we should not speculate whether the future will see nations which are now obscure becoming technological powerhouses. Recent global dispersion of manufacturing locations and supply chains increases the likelihood that previously undeveloped areas will spawn useful technology. So far, we in the U.S., by good luck rather than by conscious management, have educated or imported enough persons of capability to do a respectable amount of new technology.

The most important story about technology is not its newness, but its pervasiveness. It has saturated the world. Even when it comes to commercializing new pieces of technology, there is often a new-and-simultaneous or collaborative development of ideas, and the ability to maintain exclusive and secret rights to those ideas is almost impossible. Astute venture capitalists will tell you that an entrepreneur who comes to their table claiming exclusive knowledge of some technology is regarded with suspicion. These modern organizers of capital know by experience that at a given time, several competing entrepreneurs are almost certainly in possession of nearly equivalent ideas. An important factor in deciding who gets the financing is the determination of the most practical approach to commercializing the idea. The mere fact that a person has the idea itself is not sufficient. It is a different developmental world than it was when new ideas sprang from the heads of a few geniuses. In the past there was far less simultaneous development than today.

The realm of competitive secrecy in the development of new technology is vastly overrated. This is particularly true for military technology, often developed over many years with many participants, such that the contributors know pretty much about the theories and designs of components and systems long before the final products are in place. The remembering public thinks back to the amazing secrecy that surrounded the development of atomic weapons in the United States (during a short period of total war). I am surprised in retrospect, but even as an adult I have never met anyone who claimed to have heard even a rumor about atomic bombs until they were actually dropped on Japan. The success of the U.S. in keeping atomic secrecy was a singular exception to the trend. This picture has changed, and most of the secrets talked about in the press are *not* secrets on a world-wide basis.

Wartime atomic development was focused in three years.

Now, two generations later, weapons programs commonly extend over many years. A major concern by their developers in the United States is the number of years of funding which can be anticipated from Congress. The technology grows gradually as these programs are executed. The real secret to their viability is the immense supply chains and infrastructure available to the United States and similar gigantic industrial powers. This is a reason one should doubt development and deployment of major new military technology by countries with small infrastructure and limited financing.

World War II was the actualization of a mass technology later called "weapons of mass destruction" (WMD). The most destructive and novel WMD was the atomic bomb program, the creation of which required the personal scientific and engineering attention of tens of thousands of people. I am unable to fashion a neat answer as to when destruction becomes "mass", and do not wish to interpret the criminality of any kind of premeditated destruction. Not enough attention has been paid to the various degrees of mass destruction possible. When does just a little destruction, say that of an artillery battery by hostile mortar fire, become mass destruction? It is hard to say. There is a German author who is receiving sympathetic reaction in his homeland to his argument that some of the air-raids conducted by the British during World War II constituted criminal indiscriminate mass destruction. It is noteworthy that the United States, having invaded Iraq partially on the pretext that the Iraqis were possessors of WMD, waged the war itself with so-called surgical precision air strikes, advertised as "not WMD". I believe that if I were trapped in a collapsing building following an air raid, I would be thinking WMD were used. Once you permit a war to start, low-level or high, it is impossible to distinguish between the methods of killing. They are all horrible.

The World Trade Center bombing, and other similar operations of war in the recent past, illustrate that technology has grown far beyond the ability of one person to kill another.

The bombing was carried out by relatively few participants, and with astronomical success. Everything went perfectly for the assailants. The planes took off on schedule, were seized easily, and flown with near perfect precision. The strike caused damage far beyond what might have been expected by even the most optimistic military planner. Because of the unexpected complete collapse of the structures, it became a superlative job. It reminded me of the fine military work done by the Japanese navy and air forces in the Pearl Harbor attack of 1941. The public has little time now, until history books are written in another century, to spend on refined analysis of military tactics. Justifiably angry, the populace is more interested in retribution and prevention.

My view is that technology now is so large, and so well distributed, that we may expect periodic disasters from humanity's accumulation of knowledge called "technology". I imagine the existence of a gigantic insurance company which has studied the total likelihood of disasters from whatever source, and created an actuarial table to allow resources to be set aside to renew the situation after those predictable disasters occur. (In fact, experts inside and outside of the U.S. government have already put a value on the probability of additional engineering failures in the atomic power plant business, and this is just one small part of the world's technological exposure.) It is probably true that the number of structures and persons in the world which can be destroyed by technology is growing at a rate larger than the rate of destruction. Although that is small comfort if you are the person destroyed, in a pragmatic sense it doesn't matter what the intent or non-intent of such disasters is. They are going to happen, and they stem from technology, not from the weather or nature, the former devils of human existence. For Society, the destruction and loss of life in the Trade Center is statistically equivalent to a big earthquake in a major metropolis. The same force earthquake which might have struck San Francisco area 200 years ago is magnified greatly when it hits today, simply because of the existence of complex systems. The success of the 9/11 perpetrators was due mainly to the existence of these systems, and if a couple of planes had happened to hit the towers by pure chance and without malice, the result might well have been the same.

Many people have consumed thinking time in evaluating the likelihood that some accident or planned event would destroy either a significant population or landscape. Such events are predicted by apocalyptic vision, worthy of the Revelation of St. John the Divine. That vision is accompanied by assumption that there will be mass death, possibly with horrible side affects, as well as radical re-constitution of what is left, with imponderable consequences. The atomic bomb had the ability to raise such fears, and whether it was a small bomb or a gigantic one, the intervening years did not diminish the world's suspicion about materials which were radioactive. Treaties, international agencies, national governmental specialists: all these and more have kept the public on edge, not just about bombs, but about any manifestation of radioactivity or hard particles.

In the laboratories and workplaces of atomic energy, there is caution, and a decent respect for the power that can be unleashed. However, there is so much to be learned, that curious researchers cannot be held back. And in the calculations of various national powers it has become interesting to contemplate the possession of nuclear weapons for specific military use.

The original atomic monopolist, the United States, has pursued 60 years of further refinement of this industrial/military technology, at immense cost. Other nations have, by general upgrading of information, acquired substantial equivalent knowledge. In addition, certain civilian side uses of the technology have evolved. By far the biggest of these is the construction of atomic power plants whose main function is to supply a source of heat which will permit the creation of high-temperature steam usable to turn steam turbines, which in turn generate electricity. In the United States, there is significant installed nuclear capacity. (Interestingly, the size and number of U.S. nuclear plants has been stable for 15 years, although the kilowatt-hours produced by them have increased by 1/3.) Some other nations . . . France for example . . . have chosen to continue with major new nuclear power station projects. Nor is this industry confined to highly advanced industrial societies. Many moderately prosperous and even marginal economies have established such capabilities. In many cases these capabilities appear to be "innocent" in that they have no military intent, but there are always fears that spread of knowledge in the field could lead to its perverse use by malefactors.

The possible ability of some one who is "not us" to mount weaponry which could destroy major world life-forms is not new, and was foreseen at the dawn of the atomic age. However, it was naively believed that the United States could control, by secrecy, the key designs and ideas, and prevent them from falling into unfriendly hands. This opinion was quickly dispelled by the competitive developments of both friends and enemies. Russia became the main known threatening force, and its capabilities led to the well-known period of 1960-1990 wherein Mutual Assured Destruction became the explicit policy of several major governments. All argued that if more than one nation had the ability literally to blow up the world, that none would exercise that ability because of the assumed "suicide factor": no one would drop even Bomb #1, in the fear that hostile reaction would provoke a world-wide holocaust.

Atomic bombs are atrocious weapons, and the nuclear power industry of questionable utility in the United States, considering its current cost structure. Better, less ecologically hazardous and cheaper means exist to support the steady growth in the need for electric power grids (or even distributed off-grid developments). The civilian part of the nuclear industry is an honorable technical off-shoot of interesting ideas in physics which germinated in the 1930's and 1940's and have since been refined. It is part of history, whether you like it or not, and must be managed. In the hands of reasonable engineering and administrative talent, I can see no reason to fear this industry, and the ability to regulate it watchfully over the next generation or two may provide some insight or radically new development which would prove constructive. At the moment it is on a plateau, suffering from a tremendous fear factor among the public. Rust-belt horror stories of Russian submarines going to the bottom of the sea with intact nuclear fuel, or leaking pipes and bad welds in power stations make the public very nervous.

It is important to note that all known alternatives to providing cheap heat are proving elusive, and of course even the use of the world "cheap" is suspect. On technical grounds, attempts to manipulate atomic power by the application of fusion techniques (as compared with conventional fission) have come up short, although work continues in that area. Solar power is an emotional favorite, but a dubious entry for major power supply. Biomass, fuel cells, windmills and hydro sources all have a small part to play where regional or special needs are involved. The big picture is that fossil fuels, (coal, oil, and natural gas) look to be the overwhelming sources of heat for the foreseeable future. Further, it appears to me that natural gas is in the lead in every way.

The continuing nerve-wracking question of military use of atomic energy still must be addressed, whatever solutions are found for ordinary civilian pursuits. The vast cost of making/purchasing and maintaining bomb-quality materials is so daunting, and should be so, to all nations, that every effort will be made to eliminate this as a military calculation. Nonetheless, because of pervasive technology which has become the world's pride, some nation or group will, in fact, make either military or accidental use of this weaponry first. Then, and not until then, the nations will react ferociously. The current nervousness of Japan about alleged nuclear development plans by North Korea is a typical case. If North Korea or some other minor power should ever deliver a single nuclear attack, it might be very helpful in clearing the air for world action. I have in mind a deep, pervasive investigation and control regime. Of course, I am speaking of one, two, three, or a dozen atomic bombs. If there are hundreds, aimed and received by multiple contestants on a world-wide basis, it will be the end, and all strategic or philosophical thoughts will be nullified.

At the moment, it is a fad and curiosity that the majority of the scientific world's expense for talent and equipment is being directed into biomedical projects. The prospects for the atom, aside from the inherent terror in what we already know, are not as romantic as thought a generation ago. The touted race into space has become routine. Advances in electronic technique, which have been a major source of economic development, are now pretty much routine, and result from private commercial interest, which continues apace. Commercial interest in satellites for communication purposes dominates much of the aerospace industry. As I write this, Lockheed-Martin has just launched a 9500 pound satellite for the account of a private U.S. media company, which will broadcast and/or narrowcast video signals to targeted audiences in the continental U.S.

The deepest scientific agenda now, controlled by budget considerations in every country, is turning toward the modification and improvement of the human body. This trend was already strong, but the hyping of the human genome, the anthrax scare, the global AIDS crisis, the aging population, and general voter nervousness about health-care above all other topics, has propelled a mighty wish list for the health field.

For a couple of generations, the massive profitability of the legal (not to speak of the illegal) drug business provided much of the scientific funding for proliferating improvements in medical equipment and technique which have led to steady improvements in life conditions. I see this profitability dwindling because of consumer pressures. The likelihood is that the Government will take up the slack if private industry reduces its research expenditures.

It is worth developing more fully the twin questions: "Who in the world sets the scientific agenda?" and "Did anyone ever set the agenda?" In the recent past, for subjects ranging from evolutionary theory to relativity, the thinking of an individual scientist, fertilized by collegial cross-interests of academic peers resulted in remarkable inventions of great merit and benefit to the world. And now . . . science is increasingly in the zone of control by (in the United States) government agencies ranging from the Office of Naval Research to the National Institutes of Health to the National Science Foundation. There are scientific advisors to the President, jobs likely to go to seasoned and therefore bureaucratized past achievers. My guess is that these persons have little ability to control the future course of research. They do have the ability to influence the allocation of sizable dollar resources, but that's about it. We are still in the reality that seminal discoveries are going to come at random, rather than be planned.

The United States government, at its inception, codified the idea of technological innovation and economic progress through the patent and copyright system. This was an outgrowth of the European notion that governments could grant various kinds of protection to true originators, so that they would be protected from commercial onslaught by immoral, mis-directed copiers and predators. Whether or not you accept this idea in principle, it does seem an improvement over the old-fashioned model of grants of monopoly economic power to friends and relatives of the King. In short, patents and their associated seals of approval and privilege are an attempt to reward merit instead of influence. The implications of these systems are now world-wide. Transnational companies in particular have valuable franchises imbedded inside the patent system, and they use those powers to restrict entrance into markets by competitors. This is not something new. Private companies have fought for and benefited by these legal rights for many products and markets. They have fulfilled the objectives stated in setting up the system, though I am not sure that society benefits proportionally.

Originally, the idea of granting patent protection was innocent. It was thought to be fair for an inventor to be able to capitalize on an idea by giving a government guarantee that for a stated period of years, no one could "steal" the inventor's idea, in which he had invested a unique effort of his own mind. Millions of patents in every imaginable field have been taken out through the years. Complex administrative machinery is required to review and control the matter. In effect, thousands of Monday-morning quarterbacks review the claims of thousands of inventors. However, the overwhelming weight of the system is no longer protecting a solitary inventor. Instead, most meaningful patents are assigned to corporations, often very big ones. Governments in general are the guarantors of monopoly by an increasing corporate network which is stretching to the ends of the earth. Further, these corporations, for good or ill, have a vast interest in using the judicial and other policing functions of government in protecting their commercial advantage.

The word "patent" is applied to hard products and processes. Customarily, such matters can be described on paper. Elaborate details are written and pictured, drawn from the exertions of the inventor's mind. A separate but closely related enterprise, the "copyright" is the privilege deemed to be inherent in the act of writing or creating a work of art. Again, governments have been persuaded that this kind of creation gives the creator a right to protection against unauthorized copying or commercial use of a developed concept. A book like this one, for example, is inherently protected against such "stealing", for a considerable period of years. In the case of copyrights the right may well be perpetuated to legal heirs of the creator.

Both patents and copyrights are subject to a large body of international protocol, and general approval of the propriety of the system. In fact, the world-wide patent and copyright system is a classic demonstration of how the world governs itself without any world government. Laying aside for the moment reservations about artificial restraints on trade, one could easily become a cheerleader for this system as one which standardizes a major area of human endeavor. Occasionally, there will be outbursts of publicity, particularly about copyrights. This is true because things like movies, music, photographs, paintings, magnetic discs, and other items with high exposure to consumers tend to be involved. Corporations do not hesitate to send in batteries of lawyers backed by government officials, even in distant countries, to enforce their rights. China was the most recent major venue for a lot of this publicity in connection with the copying of magnetic tapes. But the entire world is a vast wilderness of competition, directly involving millions of participants. The present system is a dyke with a million holes in it, where only the most prestigious ideas get into high-profile court cases.

In discussing the methodology by which technology is learned and advanced, some think that it determines the rise and fall of civilizations. An academic discipline has emerged, whose scholars study the history of technology. Partly they do this because it is intriguing work; partly there is a legitimate desire to learn what factors contribute to better technology. For example, there is a school of thought that technology improvements swept the western world after 1500 because the intimidations of religion and feudal arrangements were weakened. This thought is that only a bunch of liberated geniuses, coupled with an aggressive capitalist system, could come up with ideas both of science and engineering leading to our present prosperity and novelty of life. The slow economic growth of Africa and the Middle Eastern countries is attributed by these thinkers to structural defects in their systems and outlooks. Specifically, they lacked either capitalism or freedom from tradition, or both.

I am in awe of the mental contributions made by thinkers operating in the several hundred years after 1500, in setting the parameters which underlie our present technological civilization. They were geniuses of their time, in a world where very few persons were wrestling with the notions they extracted. As pointed out earlier, this work has now largely passed out of the realm of the individual inventor. Instead, *groups* of creative individuals, often equipped with expensive test and laboratory facilities, are almost always involved with major developments, both in basic "pure" science, as well as in engineering applications. The facilities to create new chemical compounds, study the electromagnetic spectrum, or do long-range analysis of mice and insects, are always in the hands of those with significant capital. You can't just scratch your head and lie in a haystack. Technology is specialized and complex, and requires complex structures to go with it.

Nevertheless, many nations contend with what they identify

as a "brain drain". The United States itself, though considered a world technology leader, often indulges in bouts of worry that we are not educating enough scientists and engineers, that we don't have enough facilities, enough money or people to create the new ideas which we have been led to believe sustain our economic growth. Most public companies, for example, will put out statements that x percent of their sales in a certain year are for products and services which did not even exist five, ten, fifteen years ago. The subliminal message is that we either create new technology, or we stagnate and die.

Cursory reading of scientific journals in the English language, which are the most seminal for the world at the moment, shows that there is no monopoly by any race, region, sex, or nationality in the authors of new ideas. I note the names and backgrounds of persons contributing learned papers on all the basic sciences, and I am continuously amazed at the universality of their origins. I have not seen statistics to back up my anecdotal observation, but the only region which rarely shows up is sub-Saharan Africa. Egyptians? Pakistanis? Singaporeans? Canadians?, Argentines? You will see them all, hundreds of them, working in the most exotic disciplines, and doing good work. In most cases, they are collaborating with persons or groups in countries outside their own. This, by the way, is a major obstacle to the notion that there is, or can be, secrecy in technology. The practitioners of most technological art are universalists, often because they must be.

It is inherent in the situation that only a very few specialists can exist in the narrowly defined fields of science, and those persons must seek out peers wherever they are.

I am surprised all over again whenever I hear of someone who has been locked up or censured for spilling "national security" secrets. I won't go so far as to say that there cannot be secrets. Even in the classic case of the atomic bomb, the secrets of doing the work put the main competitors (U.S. and Britain vs. Germany) only a few months and years out of phase with each other. The still-sensitive evaluation of what the scientists on both sides knew, and when they knew it, is headline news material. Secrets, if there are any, are quickly learned and copied, in science more than any other realm. For science and technology, just as with economics, we should celebrate the opportunity to transfer ideas and wealth from group to group and nation to nation. When selfish possessiveness of capital becomes a leading barrier to world prosperity, steps must be taken to free its flow.

LEISURE

I have begun to ask friends what it is that they expect to be doing with their time in the next few years—or even *forever* if I encounter a particularly thoughtful individual. While I admit that my lengthier chronological age propels such questioning to my contemporaries, I am equally interested in the response of the younger among us.

My question arises from curiosity. Are others' minds working in the same way as my own? Are others wondering how to live at ease with each other during a long period of physical weakening combined with relative comfort? What is the future for a civilization which has succeeded in the age-old quest for material success? The generality of humankind is living a resolutely better daily life, despite wars, diseases, and habitual human vices. Even the poorest of the poor, though separated from the rich by a great gulf, are steadily making statistical "progress" in their material condition. People have access to machines, shelter, and food resources unheard of 100 years ago. Famine and drought and disease are diminished.

None of us can look simply to economics or technology for an explanation or a prediction of what happens in the world. Anyone familiar with "Chaos Theory" as currently propounded by physicists, understands the ability of very small events to initiate profound and novel consequences. Thus I am quick to acknowledge that a small person, idea, or passion could upset all the reasoned logic of our current world system of ideas.

Of course an outside observer might question the assertion

that our civilization has "succeeded", and could point to many social distempers. But I will stick with my notion that the general outline of success is there, which was not the case one or two hundred years ago. This success has led to such developments as:

- World-wide abandonment of agriculture, and re-settlement of many agriculturalists into cities.
- Spread of capital facilities to all corners of the globe
- Growth of structures of government and commerce
- Improvement of the status of women
- Universal use of energy sources to power machinery

Each of the above topics warrants volumes of writing and explanation; all contain a common ingredient, which is the growing efficiency in the creation and distribution of goods and services at relatively low cost. To be sure, we all complain, and I suppose will always do so, that this or that is beyond our means, that the rich get richer and the poor get poorer. Thus we quote, as our fathers and mothers did, aphorisms which emphasize life's never-ending struggles for everyone. But overall living conditions, with some exceptions, are getting better. Masses of people have more time away from the labor of feeding, clothing and housing themselves than at any other time in history.

Beginning in my lifetime, social observers began to analyze what these masses were going to do with this new "leisure" time. An industry was defined, from bowling to barbecue, which described the activities which would fill billions of minutes wrung from the occupations formerly required to live, from gathering fuel to digging ditches.

A big part of the efficiencies which bring us to this stage of leisure can be assigned to the standardization of production. Raising salmon in controlled fjords gives you better product with less waste than sending out brave men in small boats. Prefabricated houses reduce building labor hours per house. An electric clothes washer is a blessing to a housewife's back and time. The logistical successes of retailers like Wal-Mart and McDonald provide tremendous cost benefits for the broad population. And yet . . . the human spirit resists the very standardization which is conferring this benefit. Henry Ford said that he didn't care what kind of color car people bought, as long as it was black. Even he, the high apostle of standardizing, ultimately had to compromise his opinion, and we were led to adopt the infinite-option car.

Social tensions have arisen because the low social cost of standardization has freed time for new activities. Such activities are scrutinized by others, leading in some cases to editorials, hand-wringing and sermonizing about improper use of leisure. I am not enthusiastic about denouncing anyone else's use of leisure time, whether it be watching TV, scuba diving, or going to Las Vegas. I *am* enthusiastic about discovering how people can reinforce their own natural interests. There is a great underlying desire among humans to possess and enjoy things and ideas which are just a little different from everyone else's.

The desire of people to be different will cause society to place an ever-higher valuation on individual artistic and intellectual creativity. The activity of creation offsets the intellectual numbness of standardization, and it is not just my grandchildren in kindergarten who need to draw and sing. For all of us, these creative arts will be the sound underpinning of the civil society of the future.

The universality of the arts has been known forever to connoisseurs. In the modern age, there is new sympathy and appreciation for the cross-pollination of cultures provided by artistic effort. Appropriate preservation and encouragement of that effort has become a recognized part of organized life. Sometimes this trend leads to excessive legalism and particularism, as evidenced by fights over who controls works of art. Nations are placing more and more restrictions on removal of artifacts from their territory, and demanding return of works which were removed by outsiders by theft or neglect. Probably the most famous case is the Elgin marbles, but there are many others. I cannot get very excited about nationalistic claims to past or current works of art. Instead I praise the efforts of people to accumulate them and use them as teaching tools in museums or even in private venues. On the other hand, I think harshly about a Stalin or Madame Mao using art as political force. It seems ridiculous that there was a strain of European thinking which encouraged art as a necessary tool of a new age. This reached a high point of development in the Mexican muralists, who clearly put their talents at the service of revolution.

While most humans have creative urges which need to be exercised, the number of those who will make famous contributions is limited. The judgment of what constitutes good art is infinitely complex, and we can all cite cases of artists who have starved and been ignored during their lives, only to be glorified at some later date. I am not arguing that the overall creation of art works of high quality will change much, proportional to the population. But I do feel that many more people, with the time and energy to do it, will participate in the arts. Philadelphia is merely a part of the trend when it re-names a section of South Broad Street as "The Avenue to the Arts". At the moment, this one-mile stretch of downtown city includes theaters, studios of dance, galleries, the University of the Arts, and two major performance halls. There is more to come, and the powers-that-be believe that a thriving arts community in the center of the City is essential to civic success. Figures from arts-supporting groups state that more people attend and pay money for participation in formal aspects of the arts than patronize professional sports.

I approve of acts of artistic creation, and also want to encourage skilled artists to do their work by making it financially possible for them to devote serious time to it. Once popes and princes were the source of financing, and often of inspiration. Now it is our democratic obligation—something we have to learn—to encourage the arts by commissioning those with talents to produce a flow of individualistic works.

I concluded long ago that I had not been blessed with the talent, or learned the discipline to go beyond being a person of average artistic creativity. Nevertheless, I took a few opportunities to learn about the process that is involved in supporting the artistic talent in others. I wish in retrospect that I had done more. Only because I had the inclination as well as a few extra dollars, was I able to discover the joys of this important function. When the commissioning of art was the province of the financially mighty, they hired architects and artists/artisans who executed the buildings and furnishings which now cause millions to visit with widening eyes the palaces where formal beauty is still contained.

Though neither king nor pope, I nonetheless had the occasion to ask artists to do particular pieces of work, and negotiated the terms of collaboration and payment. I learned something about that procedure. In all these cases, the work was two-dimensional graphic art, but I feel certain that the same emotional arrangements would pertain to sculpture, music, books, or other fine art. In all the cases, the artists were people I had come to know through some social circumstance, and they were people either at the beginning of artistic careers, or at least naïve enough to have discourse with me about the projects. That is to say, as I will illustrate further, these were not artists sent to me by galleries or agents; they were not socially or artistically famous persons.

Once I had accumulated enough assets to consider the cost of artistry, I made a relatively foolish, yet necessary initial step into learning the ropes. A friend called to invite me to participate as an "angel" in putting up money to support the commissioning and production of a Broadway play. He was the playwright, and had a rising reputation. I was not wrong in judging that he was a superior talent for the New York stage, and he is today, many years later, a highly respected veteran of theater and film. Nonetheless, the play opened and closed the same night. My investment disappeared, and I was bereft of dreams of mixing in that romantic life. The lights, the action, the roar of the crowd all died down, and I had a file folder to show for it. Certainly this was a good outcome in learning for me. I discovered that the arts can also be a business, subject to the world's ancient risk laws of profit and loss. One of my daughters, a professional musician for many years, can attest to the fact that artists do not generally get rich. There is nothing new in that. However, this episode was merely a financial gesture by me toward a world which I wanted to enter, but to which I was not offering talent. Instead I had merely the money to take a small part. Even if the play had been an immense success, I would have been a tiny stakeholder in a financial venture, with no direct contribution to the creative output of the writer, actors and producers.

So much for an aborted venture in group financing of an artistic enterprise! Within a few years thereafter, I took an initial foray into one-on-one commissioning. I had met a group of people in a part of Philadelphia frequented by artists. Only ten miles from home, the city's Fairmount section was enjoying a renaissance of 20th century gentrification, far different in character from the regularized suburban landscape where I then lived, and still do today. It was the neighborhood—very genteel in the late nineteenth century—where my grandfather had grown up. After years of decline, it had taken shape as a haven for intellectuals, artists and professionals. It was a coincidence that one of the most famous American artists, Thomas Eakins, lived over a hundred years ago in the same block as my grandfather, and it pleased me to think of this area as a renewal of an honorable center of intellectual activity.

I had begun to love the ambiance of Fairmount's 19th century mixed architecture, which in Philadelphia's rectilinear arrangement was about 8 blocks by 12 blocks. It had emotional content for me, and I wanted to capture something about that against the day when my friends would be scattered and the enthusiasm dimmed. I started a conversational search for an artist to do what I had in mind.

Enter M. X. Chen, a Chinese refugee from Mao Tse Tung's Cultural Revolution, who had been encountered in China by a

Princeton woman. She was impressed by his artistic talents, and arranged a scholarship for him to study at the Pennsylvania Academy of the Fine Arts. He took up meager lodgings in West Philadelphia. When I met him, I was impressed, and looked at his portfolio of previous work. I decided he would be a good person for my experimentation, as I refined what it was that I needed.

"I cannot say what I want you paint," was my statement, as we began to talk about the commission. He had never seen this neighborhood, had lived in Philadelphia about 6 months, and had come directly from the rice paddies of central China. "But I want the painting to be big, because I have high ceilings and big rooms, and my taste runs to big things, not tiny things. What I would like you to do is to walk through the area, and look at it as an artist, imagining scenes that you think catch some spirit of the 150-year old residences." I told him that I wanted a remembrance, and it could be one of many possibilities, but that I craved one detail. I wanted at least one doorway which had the characteristic white marble arch used in the doorways of most houses.

Chen was self-confident. He walked through the area—purposely not accompanied by me, although I outlined the boundaries. In a couple of days he produced some little sketches, maybe 8 inches by 8 inches, and we discussed the merits of the various scenes he had found engaging. He defended his ideas, and we decided to go for a certain street scene, which has hung upon my office walls for 20 years now, to my continuing pleasure. As a student, Chen had done oil paintings of perhaps 2 feet by 3 feet, but I demanded something in the range of 3 ½ feet wide by 4 feet high. This turned out to be a surprisingly challenging learning process for him. He had never done such a large piece.

What I learned from the encounter was how to give an artist proper scope, and yet proper direction. I found the one-on-one dialogue fruitful, each one gaining knowledge and appreciation by the exchange, and I resolved then and there to do more commissioning in the future.

Through the years I accumulated an antipathy for all the male head-and-shoulders portraits which dominate socially acceptable Philadelphia. I suppose it was the Union League which shoved me over the edge with its rows on rows of men in oils, but there were plenty of other places where I saw infinite portrayals of men, and few, if any, of women. It kept growing in my mind that I should commission a portrait of my womanly wife. Was it the measured rectangular sameness of the male portrait galleries that drove me to think that I wanted an oval portrait?

Keeping my eye out for the proper solution, I inquired among the usual sources: galleries and friends. I discovered that Trish Karter, a friend of one of my daughters from her college days, was painting portraits in Boston. I had liked her personally, and now quickly came to the point. In this case I had to satisfy three demanding personalities, that of my wife, the artist, and myself. The artist came, took a look at Mary Liz, whom she had known for years, and expressed her enthusiasm for the project. We explored oval compositions and framing, and decided that my enthusiasm for that would have to be dropped. It would be rectangular, and Mary Liz would come to Boston for a couple of days of sitting and being depicted. We agreed on the style in which she would dress, and then I left the matter to the two of them. The result hangs in my office, and I often think of Trish's cocky statement from that time: "Buck, you are not just getting a portrait, you are getting a *Karter*." I loved her outlook. She has since become a businesswoman of significant stature in the Boston world. No more portraits . . . and that is too bad!

Lastly I relate the development of the Buck Scott/Canusamex book plate. In many ways this was the most entertaining project of all. Again, this is a plea to readers to investigate, commission, and collaborate with artists to do work and create beautiful things. You can buy standard book plates to paste into your personal library treasures. People have done that for a thousand years. You've seen them: Pictures of ships, or cozy library fireplaces, with the expression "ex libris" and a place to have your name printed. But, ah, to have your own specially designed book plate! That is a challenge, and one that puzzled me for some years. I decided that I wanted an *engraved* plate, not just a plain old printed thing, and I did not have the faintest idea where such a thing would come from. Inquiries to book stores drew blank stares.

One day I saw a calling card posted on a bulletin board in the small print shop where I do business, and the card advertised engraving services. I investigated and found a young man who had fallen in love with engraving, and maintained an ancient engraving press in his basement in Havertown. I also found, by consultation with Roger Moss at the Athenaeum, that there was a giant book plate collection at the College of Physicians and Surgeons. I had discovered, serendipitously, the province of kings and dukes, sheikhs and maharajas. What was a casual desire of my own, turned out to be the pre-occupation of a class of wealthy patrons, all of whom went to extreme lengths to provide themselves with unique calling cards for their beloved volumes. I sat in the Physicians' library for several hours, amused and entertained by hundreds and hundreds of fancy bookplates.

The result of this, after several months of preliminary design and a lot of hard work by my new friend Richard Wagner, was 200 copies of a book plate that was so interesting to me that I hated to paste it in most of my books. We met in his living room, we discussed designs. He made suggestions. I did. He engraved. I found sources of information. We both learned, and this confirms my wish to get another commissioning project under way . . . soon! There *is* value in a passive participation in leisure artistic activity. I am not a harsh judge either of how people learn, or what they learn, and I am willing to admit that a majority of those who attend operas, art museums, football games and other entertainments are essentially passive participants, while a few are enthusiasts. Compilation of football statistics or knowledge of opera themes are positive contributions to the mental health of the practitioners. Knowledge acquired from television or the Internet is equally valid with knowledge acquired in a formal classroom. Nonetheless, the vast increase in time available for informal education among the adult population raises vital questions about the main trends in use of these optional pursuits.

Education for life is a theme that grows in importance every year, as leisure time is capitalized by millions who comprehend that their satisfaction will grow in proportion to their education. The soaring enrollment in community colleges, the popularity of adult education as a major component of institutions which formerly catered only to the young, and the increased requirements for re-training and advanced training of workers within the existing commercial and governmental structure are all major indicators of our continuing belief in the power of education. The critical difference now is that all ages are involved in this.

At the outset of my life, education was provided mostly for the young, by a human teacher, aided by tools which had evolved over the ages, but which had not changed much. Books and papers were the principal operating tools, aided by a few mechanical gadgets such as blackboards. A hundred years of telephones did not change that pattern very much. With the inauguration of TV, however, there began to arise claims that a teacher could, at little expense, bring teaching power to thousands of viewers/listeners. These claims covered both direct formal instruction, as well as indirect general dissemination of information. I think many of these claims are justified. Populations throughout the world have moved gigantically in their general as well as specific comprehension of thousands of subjects.

At the start of the TV Age, little attention was paid to the essential passivity of the TV medium. In a way, TV talking heads were like the traditional method of teaching in classrooms through the whole world. That is to say, a teacher stood in front of a class, perhaps with a pointer or chalk, and declaimed whatever subject was assigned, while students took notes or otherwise absorbed a certain percentage of what was being said. Americans were thought to be unusual in encouraging interactive relations between student and teacher, with much questioning back and forth, as well as generally more unruly classroom situations.

My own analysis of this question of how one teaches was

delayed for many years because I was the beneficiary of teachers at Haverford School and Dartmouth College who, I thought at the time and still think, were superior beings whose offerings of information I was glad to absorb. I didn't wish for any better, and did not think much about the system, or the concept of teaching, until much later in life.

The simplistic idea of a teacher appearing in front of a class was stylized at the universities of the middle ages when lecturing began to predominate. Later on as organized secondary schools emerged, the "classroom" became standard. It may be that this concept will be further modified in future.

When I was young and attending Haverford, I was accustomed, whether in Latin, Physics, or History, to a class size of about 20 students, and a very good teacher (in those days mostly men). I recall listening to my father, a trustee of that privately-operated school, relating at our dinner table that he had been trying to persuade the financial people at the school that they could increase its teacher/student ratio from 20:1 to 21:1. (I have forgotten the exact numbers, but the point is that my father was trying to stretch that ratio upward . . . probably to squeeze more teaching out of a fixed money budget). I am now in the camp of those who believe in budgets that support small ratios, and even smaller ratios where particular social or personal problems prevail among students. To me, it is wrong that the high school in my prosperous town has a ratio of 25:1, while the high school in Philadelphia city has a ratio of 40:1

The idea of a teacher controlling, much less educating, 40 pupils . . . of any age . . . is ludicrous, and yet politicians arise with straight faces to describe what a bad job school X is doing in preparing its pupils to be useful, educated citizens. My perfect picture of a classroom is one in which there is a teacher and five to ten students.

Another component of teaching has to do with equipment, or aids to understanding. I am fond of quoting the learning procedure accompanying the study of celestial objects in a planetarium. Historically, the Zeiss optical company first designed machines which would accurately shine on an overhead dome the position of stars and planets, and correctly show them rotating or wandering through an artificial night sky. If a student sat in such a building and looked overhead, he duplicated the view he might have seen seated in a pasture located on the earth's surface. Now, newer machines are based on the idea of showing the galactic universe as though the viewer was seated in outer space. This is a classic statement of a thought in teaching that was almost unthinkable . . . equally thrilling to both teacher and student. We find it hard to imagine the arguments between Copernicus, Galileo, and Church authorities: is ours an earth-centered solar system or a sun-centered one? Yet until the space program started, no one even thought of how things would "look" from a position not-on-earth.

Albert C. Barnes died in 1951. I never met him, but from studying his written works and his marvelous art collection, I perceive that he was teacher-in-chief. He was a rich and famous collector of French impressionist paintings, African and American handcrafts. Not only did he collect, but he built a fine museum to house his art in Merion, Pennsylvania, and dedicated it to teaching art, its methodology and its appreciation. The Barnes collection and its legal saga is the stuff of world-wide art world gossip down to the present, still being played out as I write this. Mary Liz attended the 2-year course of lectures offered by them, about 30 years ago, and her involvement has been a lively component of discussion in our circle of friends. Barnes and his disciples developed theories of art about which they have published numerous books. I am not an expert in his theories, though I love the Barnes collection, and go there as often as possible. However, I am fascinated at the audacity with which he and his successors have maintained that art should be studied, not just looked at in a casual way. Barnes's ideas have gotten much local publicity in my lifetime, starting with the program instigated by Walter Annenberg to break the provisions of the Barnes will by allowing the general public to visit the collection. Annenberg, acting editorially in the Philadelphia *Inquirer*, which at the time he owned, conducted a campaign which induced the Attorney General of Pennsylvania to force modifications in the arrangements under which the collection could be viewed by non-students (i.e., tourists and casual guests).

I started to think about the intricacies of museums and their educational purposes as a volunteer at the Franklin Institute. This non-profit organization of distinguished scientific, engineering, and promotional lineage, is now mainly a museum, catering to the mass market for general science education. Still a very fine museum, the Franklin was once unique on the American scene, a true pioneer in science education. Now, most American cities of any size have very good science museums, which are a great benefit for public instruction.

In the 1970's, we were making major studies and changes in what we were doing and why. I began to think about the place that museums play in the American educational experience. I watched the hundreds of school buses lining the streets near the Franklin, pouring out kids who tumbled through the building, doing interactive experiments, watching films, walking though fiberglass hearts, etc. I listened to Nobel Laureates who said that the introduction to science provided by the Franklin years ago was an opening to their life in science.

As a microcosm of American civilized urban life, Philadelphia has many museums, both specialized and generalized, some of a recondite character seeming not to have any connection with the education of the masses. One such is the Rosenbach Museum, a repository of rare books and manuscripts. We have patronized this institution, because I feel duty-bound to support cultural efforts of this kind, where there is no generalized fiscal support available. In effect, this puts me in the lineage of those kings, bishops, and captains of industry, who once thought that the apex of high culture was the collecting of fine books. Our "patronage" is financial, and minor, but on one occasion I went there and personally handled, for an hour with special gloves, a first edition of *Don Quixote*. This was a great emotional thrill for me, though I don't believe that it contributed much to my education. It is remarkable that even a rarified collection like the Rosenbach asserts that it has an educational facet to its existence. They try their best to interest the general culture-consuming public in their marvelous collection, but it is almost inconceivable that they can be anything but a specialized academic resource.

As we look at the future, it is well to admire the aesthetics of oil paintings or fine books, all of which are collectibles for a few beholders, held privately or in museum collections. Nevertheless, I find myself most interested in the evaluation of architecture, because it has such profound influence on the overall sensibility of the community. Architecture gives each region of the world its characteristic appearances and memories; looking at it and using it is a pervasive part of daily life.

It took me a long time to understand this point. I was brought up in an engineering environment: my father and his father together put 100 years into engineering, and I too was attracted to how things worked. Many questions in the commercial world specifically involve the practical application of mechanical engineering. I hope that I am more balanced now, and I look at the art of architecture with a more serious eye. Particularly, I look at it with an eye to city planning, or lack thereof. I watched Philadelphia's re-development, and the design of major structures in other cities, and began to learn about good urban planning.

Dartmouth College, an isolated New England educational institution set in beautiful natural circumstances, became my first home away from home, in 1947. Its architecture is predominantly brick and Georgian. President Eisenhower once visited the College as a commencement speaker. He said that on looking around Hanover, he decided that this was what an American college campus should look like. (It is a coincidence that Baker Hall, its main library built in 1928, is a Philadelphia Independence Hall look-alike.) Hanover is a seasoned repository of a certain strain of architecture, different from the gothic arches of Princeton or the Tudor of Penn. I thought it was great architecture then. Now I feel that it is just comfortable.

I look at every concentration of population now to judge the architecture of its individual buildings. Then I assess its connection to the other buildings which form a community. I confess that I have moved partially away from urban planning as it exists in bureaucratic form. Planning building footprints, heights, purposes, and transportation modes is the stuff of current city development. This planning adds to the difficulty of making distinguished design. I have long lived in a clean, organized suburban setting among buildings that are legacies of the early twentieth century. I had no sense of design then, and was content to believe that we had such a nice homogeneous community because of "zoning", which kept the gas stations away from the factories and the big houses away from the little ones. I didn't care that the shops and commercial signs were ugly. If I cared at all, it was in appreciation of the residences. Now I would love to have a handsome school building and library, or a lovely theater. I care about the appearance and placement of parks and playing fields. It must suffice that I walk around a largely residential neighborhood with single houses on lawn-dominated lots. I evaluate the details of these buildings, contributed mostly by architects, builders, and owners now gone. I study colors, patterns of stones, pitches of roofs, arrangements of windows. Landscaping, too, plays a big part in my judgments. Over and over, I see ruined arrangements, spoiled by mechanical things like compressors and evaporators, ugly utilities, meters, cars and trucks, garage doors. This conjunction with the reality of modern engineering is bad enough outside, but inside it is often even worse. I sigh, and move on to larger houses, built for the economically mighty, who presumably hired capable artists to design their homes. The picture here is better, and we now have campaigns to save some of these remarkable structures. Many have been turned into schools, churches, or group retirement homes, and in our community, at least, preservationist thinking is strong. However, in the whole of Lower Merion Township and Narberth Borough, I cannot think of one case of a building made in the last 50 years with distinguished architectural features. There are cases of excellent re-work, such as the Admissions building at Bryn Mawr College, but not much of note. And this is in one of the wealthiest communities in America.

As a young person, I had the nerve to tell Katherine McBride, then president of Bryn Mawr, that architects generally put together public buildings which were OK to look at but did not work. The topic of our discussion was a dormitory designed by Louis Kahn, later built and still extant. Within the first few years after its construction, important mechanical and electrical systems from plumbing to exterior walls failed. I grew fonder of the design, but admitted to myself that it was an engineering disaster. Again in the brashness of inexperience, I went to examine the Kaufmann residence at Fallingwater. This home, deep in Pennsylvania's Appalachian forest, is an icon of American design done by Frank Lloyd Wright. Although I admired the design, again I found it did not work. It had many features which did not resonate with me as a potential occupant. And as I learned more about the glories of current architecture, I visited the Kahn building at the Salk Institute in La Jolla. I was astonished at how beautiful it was. I still have a picture in my mind of the gorgeous white marble building overlooking the Pacific, but I was not able to query the working inhabitants as to what they thought of it as a practical research laboratory.

Cathedrals are another category of large public buildings accounted to be architectural masterpieces, and I have visited my share of those: Notre Dame, St. John the Divine, Canterbury, Seville, Chartres. Western European and American civilization is handsomely set off by hundreds of such structures. Even the worst designed are contributors to the overall sense of history which occupies the traveler's mind. But as I have absorbed the details of these buildings, I feel that their truest value is in their relationship to surrounding structures. Nor do I mean to say that all the buildings in a given city must conform or be directly associated with the surrounding buildings. That is a phenomenon attached to Williamsburg and similar reconstructions which have by-passed their actual building history. It is best seen in a city when one or more major public buildings find themselves in agreeable conjunction with a miscellany of smaller structures. San Francisco is such a case, for example. I have a different view of the relationship of architecture to society than I once did. Now, with the entire world burgeoning with structures, it will be up to skilled control thinkers to moderate the buildings in those relationships. Art Commissions, Planning Boards and the like, will ever more intervene in this, no doubt with some stultification of the true artistic impulse.

In all my view of the arts, I love to think about the imagination and fancy of creation, often wondering what sets apart the truly creative from the ordinary. I have always doubted my own creativity, and admired that of others. There is also the factor of hard work and studied technique which enters the equation. Edison, a creative mind with an engineering bent, famously praised perspiration over inspiration, and there is no doubt that masters like Goya or Van Gogh could not have achieved what they did without mammoth preparation of mind and method. The joy of creation asks that the world honor dreams. The visual artist has waking dreams of what he is about to commit to his surface. Sleeping dreams too, somehow, are the creatures that feed the future.

ORGANIZATION

How is the world organized? Many, many thinkers, often called philosophers, have tackled this question. Some of the most famous did so in past ages when the world was less known in its totality. As the modern world emerged into its present huge size and complexity, the analysis became specialized. Theologians, economists, politicians, and literary figures spoke as best they could. A few broad thinkers like Karl Marx attempted general discussion of the question, and some braved prediction about the world future.

Since an organization is an artificial device without a body, it cannot take action. It can be blamed or praised for what happens, which is actually executed by human beings. I am fascinated by organizations. Their possible perpetuity has been invested with all kinds of social potential. We have come to rely on them, and create thousands of them every day.

The manner of organization has as much to do with outcomes as any other topic, though it is tedious to contemplate. It is colorful, and less work, for a student to focus on the leadership of organizations: the president of a company, the king of a country. I was the beneficiary of groups which had grown up in the history of civilization, and took them for granted, little thinking that they could be altered in character or purpose. Later on, I learned that both kinds of changes were going on at all times. In this chapter, I study the influence of organizations in my world, which rapidly became the entire world.

As a young person, I lived in a privileged economic position:

a safe home with a close family, good financial resources, and excellent education. Early on, I became conscious of the existence of governments, and of commercial enterprises. We were in the run-up to the Second World War, when it appeared to my young understanding that the future of the world rested in the hands of the Churchills, Roosevelts and Hitlers, as the heads of their nations. There were good nations and bad nations, and that was it. Similarly, there were companies: my own father appeared to own one, and I could see that the source of money, and the objective of ordinary economic life, was the success of these companies. Of course I perceived that some countries were monarchies, some republics or democracies, and some dictatorships. Much later, I found that there were big companies and small ones, more-or-less virtuous ones, and some which were crooked or sleazy.

The big revelation to me occurred when I went into the Army, *after* all of my education and study of organizations in the formal sense had been accomplished. I then discovered the marvel of organization represented by the government of the United States at the close of its gigantic struggle in the Second World War. I found out why we won that war. We had immense resources, more than all of our opponents put together, and we were highly organized. Yes, we were somewhat wasteful, and we had a tremendous overhead which was designed on the basis of ten men behind the front to support one who was actually fighting. At first, I was inclined to scoff at the overhead, feeling that the important thing in a fight was to have more fighters, not more rear-echelon support. Later, I changed my mind as I saw what immense war-making power emerged from that vast organization.

To ponder why the United States has been successful is the task of history, and I respect the view that the nation came very close to being unsuccessful at a number of critical points. Had the French not supported us militarily in the 1770's, had the Civil War split the country, had the Germans or Japanese developed an atom bomb before the Americans did, we would not have achieved our present world status, which world opinion increasingly describes as an empire. Through all the growth and success of the United States, however, there was a steady accumulation of experience in development of a large superstructure of government. Much of this development was uniquely pertinent to our large geography and polyglot population. In Philadelphia in 1787, the founders, in amazing intellectual confluence, established the main bones of this organization. The ensuing 200 years fleshed out this work with much muscle, fiber, and complexity. Some argue that the job is complete; others think it is just starting. However it is viewed, it is clearly an immense structure.

The basic wealth of the United States permitted the development of this high-overhead, high-output government. That finally resulted also in a military power equation which put the United States in its present position of secular power. Now we have grown accustomed to large governments, here and elsewhere, because much of the structure required to run the U.S. has been partially replicated elsewhere.

We also know that organizational development has spilled over into other areas of human endeavor that are not governmental: companies formed for the conduct of private business, religious and social organizations. As in most matters of the current world, there is an on-going trend toward bigger size for such organizations.

My study of organizations begins with the planet as we know it. Part of my thinking is theoretical generalization. Part is detailed description of how organizations are set up at present. Part is my guess and hope for the future . . . a future beyond individual control, yet which is also subject to natural forces and conscious decisions.

In either a critical or approving tone, many communicators endorse my opinion that there is a new organization on the planet, called the U.S. Empire. The idea has been around for years, but gained weight after the political collapse of the Soviet Union, and the development of the thought that the U. S. had become the "indispensable nation". Or put another way, many thoughtful people felt that if the U. S. didn't exist, it would have to be invented. Financial crises happened in the 1990's in Latin America, southeast Asia, and Russia. When these events occurred, nearly everyone threw up his hands and called for assistance from the Americans.

By the late 20th century, it was not military problems, invasions, or destruction caused by wars which caused major dislocations. To be sure there were still de-stabilizing small wars, but in the big picture these were not as overwhelmingly influential as the two world wars had been earlier in the century. In the last 50 years of the century, the *threat* of war involving weapons of mass destruction was much more dominant than its actuality. It became only the U.S. which had in place the financial resources and skills, plus the raw military machine, to bring together packages of money and other incentives to calm frazzled nerves. By this time, despite the attempts of Europe to create a leadership bloc, and despite the heroic growth of China and continuing prosperity of Japan, most financial and political leaders throughout the world *wanted* the U.S. to cause solutions, either through private or governmental devices (Commercial banks, International Monetary Fund, World Bank, World Trade Organization, etc.) Stability of prices, employment, and the stability of regimes both good and bad were at stake throughout the world. Textbook arguments about whether governments can or should be able to control megadiastrophic world conditions were put aside, and the United States president and administration stepped in to take the blame or praise for the outcome.

In the 2001 aircraft suicide events, the U.S. was physically attacked by a novel military tactic. This was portrayed as "War" by the U.S., and not denied by the attackers, who themselves declared the U.S. to be an imperialist, hegemonic would-be empire. A U.S. president described the antagonists as "an axis of evil", and it is still being debated whether there is an organization involved in it. (The word 'axis' was applied to the relationship between Germany, Italy, and Japan versus the U.S., Britain,

France, Russia during the Second World War, but I've never seen credible evidence that there was any close co-operation between Germany and Japan. Each was then advantageously pursuing its own separate, old-fashioned agenda.)

The word "empire" is now on the table openly, being debated and refined. My view is that it is a justified claim that the U.S. constitutes an empire, but it is a different kind of empire than those known previously. We are certainly contributing to novel arrangements, and perhaps to some major organizational changes and improvements. Most observers are still seeing "empire" through a lens of military action propelled by power politics, including colonization and control of land and other assets. This pertains particularly to the politics of oil, in which it is a cliché that governments make most of their moves over the control and ownership of petroleum.

If we accept the notion that the U. S. has an unquenchable thirst for the goods, services, and commodities it is possible for the world to provide, then all countries of the world are going to regard it as the ultimate, deep-pocketed customer. The most up-and-coming huge country in the world . . . China . . . believes this so much that it runs a gigantic export balance-of-payments account with the United States. This in turn adds to our already large existing payments deficit with the rest of the world. It puts heavy pressure on the U.S. for a fall in the international value of the dollar, and the only amazing thing about that is that the dollar remained "hard" during a decade of heavy imbalance, with its weakness only starting to show up in 2003. I inject this discussion of the dollar to illustrate its bearing on the question of whether the U.S. is an empire or not; in fact, the gross international trading dollars involving the United States, whether they are in surplus or deficit, absolutely dwarf the activities of almost any other nation or combination thereof. That lends credibility to the idea of the U.S. as the indispensable nation. If it is indispensable, then its actions or inactions on the economic front alone make it kind of a universal insurance company which nobody in his right mind wants to put out of business. I regard that as a fact, and as confirmation that the elements of empire are in place: nobody dares to tackle the empire, or its imperial leaders, except at the margins.

Those who think of empires in the old-style way, as being legions of military, religious, and commercial occupants of other peoples' countries than their own (e.g., Britain) have a tough time thinking about a non-military empire. But wait . . . just as our trade volume dwarfs anything else in the world, our military expenditures do, too. Whether we use them for politically-correct purposes, whether they just sit and wait, the absolute and ruthless force that they represent means that we do indeed carry a big stick: another confirmation of the existence of an empire. The final element of empire, however, is not yet supplied. What is missing is any coherent ideology to charm the spirit and keep the citizens of the empire contented, if not docile. Until there is a general ideological agreement about the nature of this new empire, it cannot be completely legitimate.

Let's leave the question of empire for a moment, and look at the main other governmental units which exist in the world. Have they changed? No, but they are bigger in terms of the populations served, and therefore in absolute numbers and in complexity. The existence and sovereignty of nation-states with agreed-upon borders has pretty much become a fixed situation in the 20th century, as compared with the fluidity of the 19th and prior centuries. There are marginal split-ups (almost no mergers), and the States have learned to send out surveyors and fences and border guards to mark the boundaries. It is not possible to describe the cultural souls of the 191 nations which exist. True, there are plenty of nations with failed, or failing, linguistic divisions within them. China, Russia, and India all have sizable "minorities" who either speak different languages or follow different religions than the "majorities". However, it can be said that all countries are run by large and growing cadres of career governmental employees, ultimately run by a leader or small group which has achieved command status either by inheritance, force, or vote. Each country is appropriately patriotic, and its government caters to the needs of the moment, leaving statesmanship and leadership to the last minute.

Private enterprise, the seeming invariant among peoples, first really defined and thought about by Adam Smith, still flourishes despite the operations of governments. There is dispute as to where private breaks off and public begins, but there is ample example throughout the world of the prevalence of individual risk taking in the hope of gain. There is a sub-set of discussion about variations in the way such private commerce is organized, but it is fair to say that there is a boss and a pyramidal organization. In industrially-advanced countries, there has been interesting experimentation about worker empowerment and ownership, and breaking up of hierarchies. But I venture the opinion that 95% of the private companies in the world are run more or less the way they always were.

Of interest, but not compelling influence as yet, are major groups within nations classified in modern nomenclature as "non-governmental organizations" (NGO). Many of these are given attention within their own nations, and also may have a tangible impact on the wider world outside their own borders. Examples of NGO's: China: Fulang Gang (a religious movement); Germany: labor unions; England: universities; Israel: political parties; United States: Sierra Club. The French writer De Tocqueville famously described the U.S. as structurally different from previous nations because of its vast array of non-governmental organizations. This characteristic is now extending to other modern countries: it is just as common to find a Rotary Club in Mexico City as in Zurich or Cincinnati.

Political parties throughout the world include affinity groups who turn out to vote for candidates and programs according to agendas promoted by the party. They also include more or less highly-disciplined members of a party who play some organized role in its operations—what the Chinese one-party system calls "cadre", what the U.S. two-party system calls "committee members". Parties are sometimes deeply imbedded in governments and sometimes are outside of the actual day-to-day government. From a global perspective, however, they are NGO's in that they are *not* the government as seen by other nations.

The League of Nations, and later the United Nations, were the first serious attempts to have a formalistic world governmental structure. Of course, there had been arrangements to do the world's business for thousands of years, but these were the first attempts to involve all nations and their governments in a system of interrelationships of a continuing nature. The United Nations' tenure was thought to be perpetual, like that of a limited liability corporation, but its sovereignty was carefully denied. It was *not* called the United *Government* or anything like that, and those who negotiated its charter carefully deferred to the nationalistic ethic with a two-level approach which has continued to apply up to the present. That two-level approach is (1) each member nation (now virtually every nation on earth), is given a seat in the General Assembly, and (2) Five of the most populous and militarily powerful nations have permanent membership and veto power in the Security Council.

There was no attempt at the United Nations to confront the obvious problem which would be involved in setting up a sovereign world government, and there is no general public discussion about this today. That problem is the apportionment of resources and control in relation to population. On the known facts, China is overwhelmingly the most populous nation, with India close behind, and with Brazil, the United States, Russia, Japan, Indonesia, and Mexico being some of the less populous but still significant influences. Nor was any attempt made to make distinctions on the basis of land area controlled by members: vast Russia and Canada were treated the same as smallish Egypt, although in the case of Russia, as a concession, seats were added for Ukraine and Belarus, (then part of the Soviet Union). There were those who complained that granting seats to former British and French colonies was a case of geographical extension of lines of political influence. However, whatever complaints existed at the outset, the intervening years have established that there are 191 nation states with generally accepted borders and generally accepted regimes.

Even in aggravating disputes and wars (such as Kashmir, Palestine, Iraq, Ireland, Vietnam), the scope of borders for the territories involved has been surprisingly static. Examples abound: Czechoslovakia, created as an afterthought to the Austro-Hungarian Empire, has in recent years peacefully split itself into the Czech Republic and Slovakia, but no one seems to have expressed territorial ambitions about adjacent countries like Poland or Hungary. Kashmir might or might not be part of India or Pakistan, or an independent country, but its overall border seems stable. And when I make the claim above that the nation states have "generally accepted regimes", I do not mean that these regimes are necessarily generally *approved*; in many cases there are substantial forces inside and outside the nations which would like to replace one regime with another. But in general, the idea of a nation and a regime within that nation, is built into the international system.

The United Nations Charter was ratified in 1945. The United States Constitution was signed in 1787. An earlier U. S. regime signed the peace of 1783 with Great Britain and governed the country from 1776 until the first constitution was adopted. Much has been made about the wisdom of the writers of the U.S. constitution. They adopted a scheme of government which provided balanced powers among the 13 states, but also supremacy of the federal government. Some proponents of the United Nations, at its founding and since then, argued by analogy that the UN's Charter must ultimately be changed to convey supremacy to the world's government. These advocates have not received much of a hearing from the world's member nations.

There is a provision in the Charter of the UN, that under certain conditions, a new world conference could be called to re-write the Charter. There has been some call for this but no enthusiasm has followed. My feeling is that there are few governments who want it, and those who do are mainly motivated by distrust of the veto power of the five permanent members of the Security Council.

The time may come for re-consideration of the source of the powers of the United Nations. This need has slowly ripened since the original disputes about powers of the Security Council and General Assembly which arose most tellingly during the Korean crisis (1950-53). As this is written during the yet-unsolved Iraq crisis, a broadening audience is studying who is directing the United Nations, and upon what authority. Even forces within nations who are enthusiastic nationalists can upon occasion wish there were a more coherent international body.

At the moment, each nation designates an ambassador to the UN, and often assistants, thus treating the UN as a separate sovereignty or foreign power. In the United States, and I suppose in all other countries, these ambassadors are political appointees of the national regime, and receive their instructions for action or inaction from a legitimate source in the regime. Those appointees are not "representatives" with discretionary powers. They are agents, and bound by the instructions they receive from their masters. Those masters can hire and fire them at will. For example, the Mexican ambassador to the UN was recently replaced overnight because of a political peccadillo (he offended the U.S. in a political speech).

Looking forward, it seems to me that activists and thinkers should be working on plans to revise existing patterns of representation within the UN, leading to representative, directly-elected individuals to sit within the General Assembly on behalf of individual persons residing within nation states. The organization of such a project might stagger the imagination at first, but like most human activities, unless the first step is taken, nothing happens. It would require more than a book to discuss the logistics and philosophy of the project, not to speak of the earth-shaking political consequences. However, I think it could be done, and if negotiation entailed an Assembly of 1000 persons, I am not scared by that number any more than by the 435 specified for the U.S. House of Representatives.

There is a curious, functioning precedent for a proportional body, right under everyone's nose, which has been quietly doing its job for many years (with occasional public flare-ups). That body is the International Monetary Fund. It operates, through financial means, the world's cross-border currency and exchange needs, which affect every nation. All nations belong to it, although it has been seen as a de-facto instrument of U.S. monetary policy, and was purposely located in Washington, D.C. Arguably, it could have been in New York, the world's financial capital, but I suppose the originators decided on Washington, in deference to its venue as the seat of the U.S. Treasury and the Federal Reserve Board.

When you examine the origins of the IMF, you find that it is a bank where member countries have contributed capital to a Fund, over the years, which can be used to stabilize currency fluctuations throughout the world by buying and selling of various currencies, and by lending currencies to countries which have temporary shortfalls in their accounts leading to potential disturbances of stability. This Bank, which in effect is a big international "kitty", is replenished and kept functioning with the substantial personnel required for these specialized operations, by the profits and additional capital flows supplied by its members. Sensibly, the Bank's ownership is delineated in terms of shares directly proportional to the amount of capital subscribed. Some of the wealthier and larger countries have put in larger percentages of capital (For example, the U.S. contributed 14%, UK 8%, Germany 9%). It seems to me that if ownership of an international organization like this can be expressed in terms of what the members put in, that it would be fair, logical, and hard to argue with, that the membership of the world's governing body (The General Assembly) should be apportioned according to population. After all, people are the world's most measurable and precious asset.

The biggest non-governmental organization in the world is religion in its manifold branches. Religion's membership and structure in many ways surpasses the size and influence of nations, parties, voluntary organizations and businesses. It has been around forever in human experience; its enthusiasms have propelled all the other groupings that mankind has created.

Among all this flowering of effort, Christianity, in all its branches, is the largest group of co-religionists. Estimates are that Christians constitute 20% of humanity, with Islam a close second, and Hinduism and Buddhism following. Many people over the last 2000 years have hoped, or even predicted, that the Christian Church had structural potential to govern the world. Early on, it acquired the trappings of empire, both at Rome and Constantinople. Significant efforts were made toward Christian governance through established churches, both in the Roman and Orthodox branches, but most of this work was superseded by secular politics, with the Church restricting itself to indirect influence and power.

Christianity's biggest competitor, Islam, arose at a later date, and soon in its various branches was associated with the aims of empire and wide-scale geographical domination. Through the centuries, Muslim monarchs ruled much of Asia and Africa. Often the areas which they ruled contained significant populations of Christians, Jews and other minorities. Muslim rulers were mostly tolerant of these groups as long as they did not assert too much political influence.

In general, Islamic rulers, like their counterpart Christians, conducted their affairs according to ancient tribal and monarchical rules. Today Islam, as a religious movement, is in charge of the national state in a few countries, but as with other religions, it does not appear to have realistic abilities as a world-wide, dominant system of thought and action. Hinduism and Buddhism, linked in their historical origins through India, spread mainly through East Asia, and became associated with the aims of kings and princes of that area, but rarely had aggressive organizing tendencies.

It is not my purpose here to dissect the belief structures of religions. I am thinking instead about their relationship to the prospects of further peaceful ordering of the world. It is not possible to evaluate the organizational potential of the world without taking this into consideration.

We see varied patterns of organization within religious bodies. Of course, belief is the starting point for organization. Believers, whether fervent or faint, constitute the membership. There is little doubt that the overwhelming majority of humanity asserts religious belief: it is a universal phenomenon or hypothesis. Once you turn your attention to the leadership of the religion, however, you see a huge variety of approaches to organization. It is important to ponder whether huge populations will be comfortable with the types of association inferred by the United Nations or other global formulations. As I write this, Iraqi Shiite Muslims are in the streets demanding that the U.N. supplant the U.S. in determining the election mechanism for replacing the structures of the former regime. That is an interesting testament to the possible legitimacy of the U.N. in one small section of the Muslim world, but cannot be viewed as a groundswell of permanent support.

In Christianity's experiments with worldly empire, the religious and secular unity of the empire was confirmed in the person of the emperor or empress, who also had a leadership role in the established religion of the realm. In the case of Islam, the rulers of empires such as the Ottoman were observers of that religion, but the religious leaders were less connected to regimes, having an independent status which is still a major distinguishing factor of predominantly Muslim nations.

Hinduism is an ancient religious agenda mainly pertaining to India, and the monarchs of various Indian regions embraced that belief over many centuries, but did not appear to use it in an empire-building mode. Buddhism arose from old India and transferred itself mostly to other Asian cultures via cultural adaptation rather than conquest. The world's most populous country, China, adopted it as a state religion. The Chinese emperor was regarded as divine for many centuries, but did not use it as a tool of imperial advancement. Japan, becoming nominally Buddhist, used it as an institutional bulwark together with Shinto as a state cult, but not as a specific imperial direction.

After the collapse of the Spanish empire in the 19th century, and the British empire in the 20th, the growth of the secular-leaning United States, and persistent Muslim separateness, the idea of a universal religion with its organizational hands on most of the world became less popular or possible than even its most fervent supporters might have wished. To be sure, there is a note of apocalyptic vision in American politics, which advances the idea that there will be a big final battle, presumably between Islam and Christianity, with the latter triumphant and ascendant. I doubt this eventuality.

Can we dismiss religion as a force for world organization? Is the Roman Catholic, Orthodox, or Protestant group a likely model for getting things accomplished in civil society, not just here in the United States, but throughout the world? How about Islam? Is it a force for stability and positive social ideas? Is it possible that interchange of information about religions will result in a new pluralism where the icons of each religion will be generally interchanged and increasingly respected? A kind of super-Hinduism? Even to raise such a theoretical possibility is to court trouble from strict sectarians. In a popular current novel called *The Life of Pi* set in modern India, the young male hero falls in love with Christianity, Islam, and Hinduism simultaneously. In a humorous confrontation, clerics from all three religions pay polite but firm visits to the parents, telling them that their son's conduct cannot be tolerated. But I think the young man's vision has possibilities.

Within the western world, Iberian, French, and British structure builders continued the ancient relationship between monarchy and geographical empire. At first, there was an expectation that habits, actions, commerce, language, religion, and other characteristics would be the same throughout the growing realms of each empire. Monarchs and their governments sent out missionaries and military/commercial enterprises to make sure of it.

By the 19th century, however, it was plain that conquest did not result in integration. Spain had success in forcing Roman Catholic Christianity on its subjects from Mexico to the

Philippines, and had pretty good luck in enforcing uniform systems of law and organization throughout its empire. Britain's empire finally failed in the 20th century because of its inability to integrate huge and diverse countries in America, Africa and India. Britain could conquer, but not convert. Certainly there had been large empires before—the Roman one being the most prominent. The Spanish, French and English empires for the first time involved all the continents, on a globe that now recognized its own limits as a celestial ball. These European experiments, now largely ended, have led to the current situation in the 21st century, where there is no old-fashioned empire left.

Modern nations have structures that are mostly secular, and overwhelmingly bureaucratized. That is to say, they have pyramidal schemes, usually departmentalized as to purpose, and the persons who fill those functions have a career in government. The functions are recognizable by others, since governments are great copy-cats, and the economics minister, the war minister, the health minister . . . all have their counterparts in the other 190 nations. The result is good for the conduct of serious business.

Individual citizens of countries are more diverse in function. They (we . . . all six billions of us) do not have any titles, or if we do, they are of a low-level and disorganized variety: Doctor, manager, professor, foreman, judge, farmer. But each of us does have an identity. It comes most completely to mind when you look at the newspaper obituaries to learn how the survivors summarize the human activity of the person who has just died. Each of us has attributes, and if those could be summarized for all 6 billion people, it would be quite a compendium of human capital.

The organizations we belong to, the loyalties we owe, the talents we have displayed . . . all are unique to ourselves, like a fingerprint, and they are capable of being cross-connected with other individuals at random.

This possibility of random connectedness is a new factor in the future organization of humanity, with many ramifications for patterns of human conduct and direction. Students of the

Internet have correctly pointed out that a major aspect of the growth of interconnectedness offered by this medium is the fact that humans can interchange information one-on-one, without it being filtered through any hierarchy. Governments are not anxious to be by-passed in this regard, and some governments, notably China, have made efforts to monitor and control email traffic for just this reason.

Another development in personal interconnectedness is the portability of one's personality. In a negative sense, people talk about "identity theft", by which they mean that a bad person steals the attributes of a good person, usually for pecuniary gain. The thief takes identification numbers, passwords and codes giving access to data, drivers' licenses, credit cards, etc., and becomes a virtual clone of another pre-existing person. This is a new type of crime, so far restricted to the sophisticated realms of finance. Nonetheless, its mere existence and possibility demonstrates that in a world of multi-faceted and anonymous encounters, there will be more and more pressure to identify and attach attributes to persons, *from birth*, which will stick with them forever. This is not just the stuff of spy stories and assumed identities. This is serious business, which will preoccupy governments in the future. I have no bias about this process from a civil rights point of view. It seems sensible to me that each individual in the world will ultimately pick up a persona which is quantifiable and storable. Further, parts of this data will be enough on the public record that direct person-to-person contact by those of similar tastes and background, will become more and more normal. One has only to look at the extensive personal dating columns of newspapers to see that it is already so, to some degree. Each person looking for a friend describes himself or herself in the most mechanistic and clichéd terms, with a post-office box as the temporary identification number.

I am troubled by this trend of life-time identification, even though I now regard it as inevitable. I am particularly worried by the fact that forgiveness, forgetfulness and mercy will go by the wayside. When I think of my own sins, which are fairly minor, I don't want any record of them. Nor do I want to have medical records going back to the Year One. Nor do I care if my friend was convicted of drunk driving. If there is one thing worse than prison, it is having all these matters put on a retrievable basis. Yet the broad social demand for "records" will, I fear, carry the day.

Aside from the possibilities for blind dating, the fact will also be that one-on-one contact can lead to creation of new organizations and organisms. For example, the creation of new political parties could well happen as a horizontal movement stemming from thousands of direct email approaches among people who formerly were neither acquainted with each other, or aware that they shared similar attributes. The recent primary campaign of Dr. Howard Dean for the presidency of the United States provides confirmation of this theory. Practically all of his money and support came from a prolific Internet campaign. While his candidacy did not succeed, I regard the phenomenon as an opening wedge for major party re-alignments in the U.S. and elsewhere. People can be as empowered by contact with other individuals as they can be by contact with groups, which after all are merely concepts.

IDEOLOGY

My family came from a line of people who had ideas, and acted on them. Many of those ideas were born in religious enthusiasm. Quakers and Baptists predominated in our family, and dissent from majority views was a habit. This was a fact made plain in letters saved from the 19th and 20th centuries and in my childhood memories. For example, as a child, I was conscious that my grandfather Scott knew African-Americans at the personal social level and was agreeable to their culture. It was a part of life that he departed from Philadelphia from time to time to visit Tuskegee Institute in Alabama. Tuskegee was the leading Black university of its day, and he was a trustee there for many years. Now it is even more famous, and I am proud of his association. I see now that his interest, and that of other leading members of our family, was definitely a minority enthusiasm.

Later, I began to learn that the Scott family had been firm in its abolitionist opinion during the years surrounding the Civil War, and this no doubt biased my grandfather's views. But this was a small part of the outlook in which I felt that we were different. We were idea people, always with something new to think about or do. My mother brought a Canadian and Anglican approach to our immediate family, and I think did not approve completely of the religiosity of the Philadelphia group, but she lived among it for 67 years. It rubbed off on her, too.

My father and mother were hard working members of the dominant socio/economic tribe in the Philadelphia region. Most people then and now would assign them to the upper 5% of society's assets and social mobility. That alone made us a minority, but in those days the words "majority" and "minority" had little political significance. I recall significant warnings from my father, when I was still a child, about unspecified dangers stemming from the possession of great wealth. In retrospect, I believe that he issued these warnings not out of envy for wealth, but rather because he himself already felt a sense of separation from the society in which he passed all of his life. Though he was one of Philadelphia's leading industrialists, he did not belong to a country club, ride horses or hunt, or present his daughters as debutantes. Deep in my own psyche is a knowledge that I too was out of step with the crowd. More light-heartedly, I concede that perhaps everyone feels some of this separation, this native desire to be different from all the rest.

Consciousness of my own identity began with my name. It is a convenient handle for discussion of self and the self's opinions, which form the backbone of this book. My name is William. So says a birth certificate and a baptismal one which followed shortly. Yet I am Buck, or Bucky, as I have been for 74 years. I share with millions of others the dilemma of having more than one alphabetical name. This is not convenient, either for me, others who wish to be in contact with me, or for the authorities. However, it is nothing new for anyone: we are all dad, mom, cousin, uncle, friend or foe to someone, and society has provided ample nicknames, personal names, nouns and titles to address the need. Yet I *do* have an official persona, particularly as I have become older, with thousands of cross-currents in my life, and I feel the need to be recognized as a particular figure. What I say, create, or hear is personal to me and me alone. As the shades of history fall, I prefer it to be clear who I am.

Recently, we were looking at examples of silver craftsmanship in the Philadelphia Museum of Art. I noticed that in the 18th century, each silversmith marked his own work. By the 19th century, many of the works were shown as being made by a company. Can a "company" make a work of art? Yes. Many famous works of visual art, like frescos, require cooperative work by more than one artist. Most scientific papers published today have multiple authors, so that it is not possible to identify a single personality with the thought. Could an individual genius like Darwin publish today? Excessive pride of individuality is a questionable attribute, which I discuss more fully in a section of the book called "Celebrities". Nevertheless, I speak for many people in asserting that I like to be identified by name. Whatever small or large attributes I contribute to, or subtract from society, I want them to be assigned to me. I am not comfortable with anonymity.

For reasons unknown to me, my great-great grandparents named their first child, born in 1832, "William Maxwell Scott", and that name has been in continuous use in our family since that year. There has never been a minute when at least one person bearing that name has not existed. Sometimes there were two or three at the same time. You can understand why I had a nickname.

I had reached the age of 50 before I decided to tackle the name problem head-on. I started to sign business correspondence, issue press releases, print calling cards, run for political office, distribute resumés under the name of "Buck". I even went so far as to create a photo-identification card for myself, because I did not want to cause confusion among those who examine passports, drivers' licenses and other lifetime documents which I have accumulated over the years. I was assured by experts that the only way for me to create an irrevocable single name for myself would be to go into court and get a legal order from a judge. This I was unwilling to do. Now, in my seventies, I am returning more and more to "William", forced by security considerations imposed by airlines, credit agencies, and the like. They are skeptical about that name: "Buck". It sounds basically frivolous!

I sketch these minor, ordinary naming problems to set the stage for a more serious discussion touching all of us on the globe. There is a trend toward, and genuine need for, a universal description system covering all of humankind. The scientific base is available to do this. (Contrariwise, the decision could be made not to identify anyone for any general purpose, and to let the sheepherder of Afghanistan continue to be unnumbered and unremembered as he always has been.) The immense hubris of identifying mankind present and future is anathema in many quarters. It is bad enough, many say, that all our existence, our sins, crimes, defaults, preferences can be stored and retrieved by awesomely huge magnetic storage. What does being reduced to a 17-digit number do to our psyches? I prefer to dodge that question.

Current United States preoccupation with terrorism leads to high-technology attempts to record the passage of travelers across borders. But this is just a small phase of the attempts of governments and organizations everywhere to identify, classify, control, and hopefully improve the individual human being. I can see no end to this trend.

Christians put a high premium on the sanctity of each individual. I am told that other religions put more emphasis on the individual as a member of a group, and Christians teach that God has the capacity not only to know each human, but to deal directly and continuously with that person through infinite time. I have difficulty with this notion, feeling that it is too exalted and complicated, and that I should seek more modest contact with Deity. I prefer to think that I can deal with the Creator, or the Creator with me, when there is something to talk about. God must be so busy that he/she couldn't possibly single me out for attention, except on rare occasions. Paradoxically, I am writing this book to identify "who I am". If this leads to a seventeen-digit number for me, and a set of biometric identifiers, so be it, but my view is that I am God's partner, trying to bring constructive thoughts and actions into life.

In many phases of living, I have integrationist tendencies. I have wanted to lead a balanced life, with all its factors interrelated. I do not want to have several sets of books for life's accounts. I try to conduct my private life roughly in the same manner as my public life. I want to treat old and young, poor and rich, smart and dumb, with an even hand. I want to be reasonably consistent, giving offense to as few people as possible, but making it plain to anyone who cares, just what my opinions are on topics of the day. This does not mean that my life is an open book. Of course I have private opinions, relationships, and confidences. My rule is that I will describe my actions, good or ill, in any forum where it is required, but life has mostly passed without such a requirement.

Some years ago, I concluded that my personal outlook could not be successfully matched with the outlook of the crowd, and also that many of my ideas were unlikely to prevail, no matter how hard my effort. This was a disappointment to me, with some repercussions in my social life. Specifically, I found that I could no longer identify myself inalterably with the stated (or even unstated) objectives of most of the groups with which I had been associated, either from birth or long adult connection. I had to live with, at last, the consequences of being that minority which I am attempting to describe.

It started with the Democratic Party, an organization I had been sentimentally linked with since the age of discretion. I had thought through the existence of "parties" in human affairs, and was and still am satisfied that such groupings are natural and necessary in the governance of humans. I was a seeker of preference in the Democratic party, spoke well of it and became a minor but hardworking partisan for it. I even perceived how I could, with honor if not profit, continue with that Party into my old age, so that my survivors could read adulatory obituaries about my allegiance to that ideology. (It *is* an ideology, albeit a shifting one during the history of the Republic.)

Particularly with the election of 2000, and then of 2002, I began to examine my personal identity as a member of the Democratic Party. I voted for the Party's candidates, particularly for Ed Rendell, who was elected Governor of Pennsylvania in a heavily-financed but intellectually lack-luster campaign. I had known Rendell slightly, liked him, and was glad to see him elected as a personality. I did not see that his occupancy of the Governor's mansion changed the components of Pennsylvania politics. In my adult experience, there has been almost no change in the make-up of Pennsylvania politics, inside or outside the parties and the government in Harrisburg.

Most observers note an increasing influence of money in politics. It has always been a factor, but the curve of spending, whether you are running for alderman or president, has gone up astronomically in the last decade. Fortunately or not, I never was in a position to spend a lot of money winning political favor or even being civic-minded. Regrettably, my personal income was never very high, and the amount available for donation to political persons or causes was small. The closest I came to being a serious player was as a member of the finance committee of friends who became members of Congress, and I think those friends were probably dissatisfied with both the size of my own contributions to their campaigns and my lack of influence in persuading others to give generously. It was simply not my game, particularly since my career occupation in the electrical power manufacturing business had little interaction with politics. The mature and private nature of that business in the U.S. provided little opportunity like that which beckoned to investment bankers, bond counsel or road contractors.

I faded steadily from the Democratic scene. I remained friendly with some of the politicians I had encountered on the way, but stopped having the opportunity to meet and work with younger ones. This was saddening for me, and I tried to analyze why it was happening. I always loved politicians as a class of people, whatever their personal views. They were more colorful and unpredictable than most people, had a public involvement which most citizens do not cultivate. Certainly the business which they undertook, namely the running of government, continues to grow in complexity and importance to society. Politicians, as distinct from the employed personnel of government, represent the unfocused aspirations of the public, and this was and is a vital component of democratic life. Why, then, was I so dissatisfied? And if dissatisfied, was there any element of that which is worth conveying?

My own withdrawal from active politics paralleled increasing withdrawal by the American public from this same scene. Voting participation continues to decline. Political platforms and principles are little discussed and mostly scorned as hypocritical and cynical. I am distantly amused more than angry, with the antics of political figures. I follow the main reported dramas, particularly in Pennsylvania, but mostly for entertainment rather than edification. I follow the attempts to form new parties which are either more focused or sanguine than the Republicans or Democrats. None of these has attracted my serious attention. I do not poll my acquaintances about their views of this, but my reading is that most of them seem to be coming to similar conclusions. A revolution has happened without any notice.

That revolution happened in a country that prides itself on its ideology. I am not alone! In past decades crowds could be moved by politics, but no more. Maybe it is just as well. The business of government is largely ministerial, is taught and learned at some fine educational institutions. From township to Pentagon, its budgets, its organizational hierarchy is well-known and quite standardized. The people who get into it are often there for life, just as in any other career zone. We are indeed part of a huge machine, created mostly in the last generation or two, which we are powerless to control, and which functions quite well. One might compare the government business with, say, the steel business or the banking business, and come to the legitimate conclusion that the only thing differentiating government from the others is that government really is not subject to competition or change. The short story is that government is not interesting at the state and local level, except as a career choice, or if you are pursuing a particular grant, subsidy, contract or other business advantage.

What *is* genuinely interesting in public life is the world of international politics, where everything cries out for attention, study, support, and new approaches. The system of nation states and their approaches to one another is Biblically complex. U.S. presidents are required by their job to have or develop a personal view of that complex subject; but when you consider 191 nations, even trying to describe the topic is a formidable task. It makes you feel sorry for the Wilsons, Roosevelts, Eisenhowers, Kennedys, Bushes and the rest: such a big job, so little time, so few people with knowledge. I am amazed at two aspects of this. First, the international system, as it has evolved, has in a creaky, cranky way, begun to work. Second, very few citizens in the United States at least, want to deal with the missing pieces. There is a feeling that it will all work out somehow, and that the details are not worth attention. Paradoxically, Americans feel that their domestic system works well enough, but feel that the international system does not require their attention. This is not only paradoxical, but also ironic, because as pointed out elsewhere in this book, there is a strong chance that the American system will actually become, or may already be the world system.

The world is a secular place, where people are mostly concerned with their own personal affairs and not socially moved much by organized religion as was once the case. The fiery mixture of Islam and jet-fuel on September 11, 2001 moved many in the US to imagine a wild-eyed Mid-East population, bent on destroying "western civilization" including the U.S., in a bath of radiation-laced, bacteria-induced poison. I do not see it that way, and I reject any concept of a "crusade" on the part of Christians, or the U.S. as a political entity claiming to represent the interests of 300 million people. Instead, I look at the world's political system as a fascinating, competitive, contentious stew of thousands of groups. The individual person needs to belong to one or more groups in order to advance his or her interests. I recognize, even though I wish some of them would go away, that the boundaries between nations, tribes, companies, unions and parties are the actual stuff of international politics. I am calm about being an individual voice not speaking as a member or a group, and I want to be accountable for each opinion that I offer. But I also believe that the interaction of the billions of beings, their hopes, fears, opinions, biases, all will result in a more livable world. I have great sympathy for individual religious enthusiasts, for politicians, for entrepreneurs . . . for all those who display their individual opinions. It is a necessary part of life to watch ideas shape and grind themselves, adjusted by the competition of their peers.

Like the generality of mankind, I am emotionally interested in the past. It is fascinating to learn about and savor the activities of ancestors, particularly if they boast a battle wound, a patriotic profile, a long pedigree, or a celebrated personality. I have taken pains for instance, to research my Cajun and Quaker roots though they were long ago and far away. And now that I am entering the last quadrant of a normal lifespan, I cannot help but be influenced by the experiences of my own life. All of these contribute to the conceit which encourages the writing of such a book as this. Nonetheless, I wake up every day wondering how to apply realistic thinking to today's situation, and try to set aside regrets for what might have been, or nostalgia for other days. Since part of my work is in the investment world, I am fond of saying that every day offers a new chance to make money. The past's triumphs and failures do not really exist. What are today's opportunities?

I like to think of myself as a realist, not a dreamer. Nonetheless, I approve highly of dreams, which I find fall into two categories: those which are hopes and visions of the conscious mind, and those which are the products of the sleeping mind. The "dreams" of public figures about their hopes for the future (Martin Luther King comes to mind) are public and often constructive. Sleeping dreams, which each of us has, are private and reflective.

I love sleeping dreams, and consider them a major contribution to my peace of mind. They are personal and experienced only by me, so cannot hurt anyone else. If they ever hurt me, which I doubt they will, I can absorb that hurt. My sleeping dreams are mainly entertaining, with a strong element of frustration and desire to accomplish things which are blocked either by myself or circumstances. Rarely have I had dreams that are frightening, and none which appear to be predictive. Sometimes I think that there is a repetitive theme to dreams which continue through the years. I have strong images of trains, often electrified; sometimes I am watching them at close range, sometimes traveling in them. I look forward to dreams in the night, and enjoy trying to reconstruct them after I wake. Mostly that attempt fails and the dreams fly. Thus I am not in the company of Daniel, who had monumental capability for dreaming in an interpretive and prophetic mode. Daniel was the ultimate dreamer and realist in his approach to Belshazzar, and I love the words he spoke to the Iraqi king: "Mene: God hath numbered thy kingdom and finished it; Tekel: Thou art weighed in the balance and found wanting; Peres: Thy kingdom is divided and given to the Medes and Persians."

The imaginings of my consciousness are the most useful and least wistful. They have been powerful at times, and enabled me to give the future a concept. Once conceptualized, I could go to work and put building blocks into place to help embody the concept. Almost never have those imaginings been fully realized, but they are occasions to permit me to bear the ordinary tasks of life with a gleam in my eye for the future. I have found out that the aggregate of ordinary tasks has all been for the good, and almost no task, once accomplished, has failed the test of being part of my envisioning. Now I feel surrounded by building blocks. Yes, the visions continuously recede into the future, bigger and less fulfilled, but still beckoning.

To illustrate what I mean, let me allude to the concept of world peace. At age 20, I determined to do something about it, and in years thereafter I worked wherever I could to further ideas that would promote peace. I did not do it continuously, or 24/7 as they popularly say today. Nonetheless, I put my shoulder to the wheel many times. For 50 years I worked at it, without major hope that I could change things in the world, simply because I became convinced that in the big, big picture there was no other subject as worthy of support. Am I disappointed that the Millennium has come and gone, and there is still war? Not really. I didn't expect success, and I am happy that so much progress has been made. The dream is now amplified; I understand far better than I did at 20 what the many dimensions of peace are. I am convinced that war as policy is a hopeless phantom, best sent by the world to the dustbin of history. I hope that I can convey some of this to others, partly to save them the wear and tear of figuring it out themselves, partly because I think I have observed some factors which may not have been noticed.

No discussion of ideas, ideals, and dreams would be complete without comment on the place of organized religion in my life. In my early years, after some initial objection, I absorbed the Christian religion. Our house was not particularly "observant", but the Scotts were Bible-quoting general Protestants, as pointed out above. My mother, out of Anglican rectitude, made sure we were participants within our parish confines. Later I added a philosophical layer with some formalistic learning at Dartmouth, and I continued to play a part in Church affairs down to the present time. I never re-read stories about Jesus without marveling at his humanity. His outlook on birth, life, death, and the human condition is so profound . . . unmatched by any other person I have heard of . . . that I am glad to live with his story. His divinity and its connection with God or the overarching physical principles of the universe is more problematic, and I do not hesitate to say that I am an unorthodox Christian. My hopes and dreams are just that. I am not thinking in terms of promises, either for now or for eternity. At times I have felt a tug toward Jewish or Quaker views that emphasize the morality of the here-and-now.

I am no more in charge of my own life than is any other human being, and I retreat from people who think they are, or would like to be, totally in control of their own lives. I have been helped by many people, often by those to whose ideas I was opposed. I have a long mental list of those who, at unexpected moments, demonstrated to me that I did not control my own life as much as I thought. My gregarious friend Perrin Hamilton, said to me: "The three most important things in life that I've encountered as a lawyer are sex, booze, and money". We often laughed over that, and I use it as an introduction to the private domain of life. It's the "good stuff" which most people, without being prurient, want to know about others. They buy books, like the one about the 20th-century public figure Pamela Digby

Harriman, to find out about the mysteries of peoples' private-private lives. Ultimately they may feel that they have found out too much, as in the case of President Bill Clinton, but there is still an appetite for this kind of information.

I have no idea about Hamilton's opinions about his own life and the *bon mot* just quoted; his opinion derived from his professional life as a lawyer, where he found that those three topics caused most of the personal disputes from which he earned his living. In my case, booze has never been a factor, except as I saw it at close range in others who were close to me. I observed the horrible toll exacted by addiction in several cases. So far booze has not been an intimate partner in our family's life. Sex and money are unusually private topics . . . probably only suitably disclosed to a confessor. It is enough to say that they have had substantial effects in my life, as they have for most people.

When I concerned myself with being a political figure, I also evaluated other politicians and their impact on voters. Not surprisingly, I found that voters wanted most to know about candidates for office: "What is his (or her) religion, age, ethnic background, and economic status?" The candidate's actual opinions about issues came in last on the list. I comprehended that average people are the ultimate realists. They want to know the things that are withheld from press releases. If he's rich, they want to know it. If she is divorced, they want to know it. And after all is said, these are some of the most important matters in a candidate's life, and interact with actual performance on the job.

Part of the leisure of life is good health, and it has been pointed out to me that the well-being of the body is a prerequisite to happiness. This is contrary to what many people imagine, but it is a school of thought that I favor. Right now, world public policy is heavily interested in health, so much so that I think it is excessive. There continue to be arguments about who is going to pay for health care. Since that care is probably the most expensive human activity one can think of, this expense, as a percentage of gross output by the world's six billion and growing population is a significant thing to think about.

My take on bodily health is most influenced by the fact that my own health has been good, so that there has been little time spent thinking or planning about the subject. I have been well fed and watered by the friendly souls surrounding me, and occasional crises of health have come only to be forgotten. The expensive and extensive medical steps taken to improve quality-of-life during the later years of existence are staggering, as we all face the reality of ever-lengthening life spans. Many friends speak to me of the wish to die without drawn-out consequences to the person dying and those who survive. But these are mere wishes and speculations. My finding is that the drive to live is powerful, even among the feeble and failing. I can only endorse the efforts of society to keep the flame of life alight. The manner and timing of each individual's passing from the world is still a mystery. It is a mystery that I prefer to keep hidden and unknown to humanity.

GENDER, RACE & CLASS

Emergence of women from the private shadows of many centuries was a major development in the world's life in the twentieth century. The importance of women to the human race . . . always a 50-50 proposition . . . did not change. Moreover, there had always been women who stood apart from the long traditional silence of family life. During my time, happily, women as a group, propelled by millions of individual decisions, suddenly grew to be a major public force, augmenting the private force they had always been. I'm happy that I lived while this was happening, and I did my part to initiate and support such changes.

I do not glorify women as a group, any more than I expect women to glorify men as a group. I content myself with the generalization that men are interested sexually in women and vice versa, a desirable universal attraction, even into old age. I cannot prove that changes in the public status of women were more important than scientific developments, television, consumerism, communism, capitalism, or any of the other major movements of our time. I can imagine, however, how this broad trend in society has directly affected the conduct of hundreds of millions of families in their most intimate relationships.

Women have always worked hard physically to support themselves and their families. Some believe that on the whole women have worked harder and longer than men. It was very little thought, however, that a woman might be paid in measurable coin, and had every right to make the decision about the disposition of these earnings. In the years between 1900 and 1999 the whole picture changed, not only in Europe and the United States, but in the entire world, even to its most conservative parts, such as Saudi Arabia. It was called "Women's Liberation" toward the middle of that period, and unfortunately became the butt of locker room and talk show humor. In reality, the foundation for this change in attitude was laid long before Women's Lib became a buzz word in the States. I will not lay out here the proof of these origins; what interests me most is the beneficial influence of this worldwide movement, down to the present day. Unless I miss my bet, no sensible woman in touch with the modern world can or should accept anything less than economic parity in society. Here in the States, women are penetrating deeper into every profession, trade, or occupation. It is impossible for me to imagine a female toolmaker, lawyer, or military officer accepting anything less than equal pay for equal work. It is still true in this country that women on average are paid less than men for comparable jobs. Bad habits and entrenched arrangements have kept us from equitable success; but the trend toward parity will continue.

The change in relationships between men and women has been a notable feature of recent world history. It now appears, contrary to the myths of the centuries, that there is no, or very little differentiation in the skills that each gender brings to society. The vital exception so far is that women have the ability to bear children. (Looking ahead, it is possible that this unique capability will be further challenged.)

I have often advised women and their male companions, of the need for capital equity among spouses or other long-range committed relationships. The reason for this is self-evident, and largely has to do with the fact that women, being the bearers and main raisers of children, may properly elect to remain outside the *paid* work force for significant periods, thereby impairing their cash operating income, as well as their likelihood of gaining competitive wages if and when they return to work. For this reason, if there is any capital in a family outside of the house and the car, partners should make sure that their savings and investments are held in amounts proportional to each partner's desire and ability to administer them. If anything, a little more in the hands of the wife would be a good direction. Each partner can then have a fair, if unspoken, self-respect as a partial guardian of the family's assets. In the U.S., most states have endorsed this concept for many years, by insisting that a house, usually inhabited by a husband, wife, and children, be jointly and equally owned by the two adults.

The inheritance of accumulated property has always been a big topic for the human race, and there are usually powerful family influences in the private disposition of capital. I suspect not nearly as much progress has been made toward equity in this field as in payment of wages or the ownership of capital which has been accumulated by the living family. Inheritances are something that affect a small percentage of families, but because capital tends to accumulate, that small group controls a high percentage of the capital of most nations. It is a social concern that such control be diluted and diversified, and in this matter and other economic policies, laws and customs protecting the rights of women need further adjustment. Although I am familiar with the topic of financial inheritances here in the States, I am only guessing at the situation elsewhere. Women everywhere have a responsibility to influence, within their own families and private businesses, the equalization of inherited capital. I cannot follow the habits and attitudes of the entire world, but my reading and listening leads me to conclude that women everywhere, probably with the approval of the majority of their husbands, are taking on the role of equals. It was always theirs, but often got submerged.

Along with increased sophistication of both men and women in understanding their income and capital comes the question of personal responsibility during the whole of adult productive life. I have always strongly urged friends that each individual does have responsibility for understanding the origins and disposition of financial resources. It is not enough for one or the other partner in a marriage, for example, to think that he or she can slough off decisions on the other. We are economic beings . . . each one of us separately, just as we are physical and spiritual beings.

But what of those adults who have no husbands, no wives, no normative long-term relationships? What of those who have different sexual preferences from those which prevail amongst coupled women and men? There have always been, and continue to be vast numbers of un-matched single, asexual, homosexual persons, living in every mode thinkable. I find these associations practical, livable, intriguing and above reproach. I wish them all well, as I do married persons.

And what of children, the blessed outcome of married life, or . . . it has to be said . . . of unmarried coupling? My observation is that children quickly grow up, they are flexible and spontaneous, sparking happiness, worry, and most of the other emotions which adults expend on their kids. In fact, the vast majority of most peoples' lives will be spent as adults, and not children. The obvious influence and training of parents goes without further description, and entire industries are devoted to advising these developments. It may sound harsh in a book written about adults and their relationships, but speaking as the father of six, I say "don't worry too much about your children". They inevitably grow up, and take their places, skewed in many of the same ways as their parents, and always providing something new.

The case of race has been linked closely, and surprisingly, with gender, in the political developments of the 20th century. Whereas race was almost absent from the philosophical ponderings of classical thinkers about world organization, it has emerged as a strong factor in the recent past. This trend might have been impossible in older days, before the advent of Darwin. By now, geology, archeology and scientific understanding of our connection to the evolution of organisms on the earth is well understood. But now, race has become a factor in political calculations. Demographic statistics exist which purport to measure how many races there are, where they are located, how they differ in character from the nation states. To some degree, speculation can occur on how races are mixing, and there is a cottage industry growing up around the very definition of race. Some scientists argue that there is no such thing, or that if there is, the comprehension of its meaning is corrupted by the public.

Race, like religion, has become much more fluid and specialized in its effect on how the world operates and governs itself. Yes, there have been clans, tribes, races and other groupings of humans defined by language and culture, for as long as mankind's memory runs. However, at an accelerating pace, these groups have so widely interbred that one becomes nervous at the job of description. Let's start with the biggest group . . . China. Many think of the Chinese as the world's largest tribe, with an immense commonality of language and habits. This is not completely the case. Not only are there significant minorities within Chinese borders, but a neighboring "tribe", the Manchus actually took over China 600 years ago, establishing the Ming Dynasty, and those outsiders are now so integrated into China that most people have forgotten this bit of history. Is there an Oriental or Asian race, and if so, does it stem from the same origins? Does it include Japanese, Koreans, Vietnamese? How about Indonesians or Malays? Would you include Burmese and Thai? There is no direct answer to these questions, which I put forward only to emphasize the difficulty of defining "race" over a long period of time.

The U.S. had a significant social problem between white settlers from Europe, and African slaves of black skin, when the former enslaved the latter. Our brief history as a nation saddled us with this unusual and charged racial confrontation, which was a rare stark event in world history. Our slaves were not able to be anything else within our borders. It's true that slavery existed, and it was not negligible, in the empires created by the Iberian peoples: Spain and Portugal. Native Americans in all parts of the Hispanic and Portuguese world, were, in effect, treated as slaves, and it was not until the independence movements of the 19th century that slavery was legally abolished, the latest being Brazil in 1888. As bad as slavery was in all parts of the world, it can justly be said that as a phenomenon of social importance, it had its gravest impact in the American confrontation leading to the U.S. Civil War and its aftermath.

Philosophers like Marx have discussed and predicted relationships related to the tensions between "classes". Both races and classes are convenient generalizing nouns for purposes of discussion. In my view, however, the vast movements of modern life are already making these concepts questionable, and these nouns more poetic than practical. There are many strategies advanced in politics and economics which relate to the "haves and the have-nots". Not surprisingly these strategies have now been extended to nations, where we want to generalize about the "North versus the South", the "Developed versus the Undeveloped".

Both class and race may be lessened in focus by the best current genetic and anthropologic work. That is characterized by a recent book *The Journey of Man* by the geneticist Spencer Wells. Wells' book maintains that a specific ancestor who lived in Africa 50,000 years ago initiated the breed of humans we now observe throughout the earth. These humans, he says, successfully competed in their surroundings, including competition with Neanderthals and other erect hominoids. Waves of his descendents moved into the other continents within 10,000 to 30,000 years, culminating in a final movement to the Western Hemisphere about 20,000 years ago. The idea of continuous competition and adaptation by the world's billions lends confirms one's visual observation of the infinite combinations of body structure supplied over thousands of years. There is no way to prove it at this moment, but it is intellectually satisfactory to me that there has been such a mixing of blood as to negate ideas which would separate the breed into sub-species or races.

I argue that there are no defined races except the human race, and no defined classes at all. However large portions of humanity disagree, and choose to make informal classifications of perception within these categories. I can't dismiss this. Every day, one can read about "race" divisions here and abroad, or "class distinctions". Here in Pennsylvania it is a commonplace to accuse a political figure of "playing the race card" in an election scenario. However, I take comfort in the notion that these distinctions are becoming less and less obvious, even to people who want to employ them for personal advantage. The vast swirl of populations over the globe is mixing humanity's former tribes at such a rate that the old racial classifications of black, white, yellow, and red are outdated. Some European-derived groups appear to be still interested in resisting polyglot trends, and there are certainly private prejudices about marriage outside the existing tribe. Nonetheless, it is striking that countries which seek most to preserve a certain purity of lineage are also most likely to disappear as entities in the next few hundred years. (Japan and Switzerland come to mind).

In doing the world's work and organizing the world's tendency to form organizations ranging from families to nation states, it has always been tempting to assign certain capabilities to certain groups of people. For example, it is plain that the world was once a hunter-gatherer world, then an agricultural world, and perhaps a manufacturing world. In the course of thousands of years, it was observed that certain groups gained specialized knowledge and other resources. Many Germans became technologists; Australians grew sheep; Japanese made clever electronics; and so on. These may have been interesting observations, but they did little to inform the future organization of the world, and the likely geographical and personal specialization of duties and activities. Even less did they inform us about changes in population density which exercise so much influence in the creation and exploitation of capital.

I further claim that there is no inherent differentiation in the skill levels offered by the broad distribution of our species. If that is correct, there is a great question as to where the populations of the world will be located, and what their principal activities will be. Should Haitians be manufacturers on a par with Germans? Is it better to grow rice in California or in Thailand? Should China be an integrated self-contained nation like the United States, or a supplier of cheap labor to the rest of the world? Probably we cannot answer these questions by fiat, but it may be destructive to leave it all to chance. Economic analysts have developed the doctrine of comparative advantage to deal with this. Without borders, but with stable populations and equal education, theoretically the world would move in a few generations to a redistribution of functions to those places where they could be done best.

In fact, such a scenario proves hateful the minute it is introduced. The idea of having all financial markets in New York City, all communications engineering in Silicon Valley, all tourism in Mexico, all mining in Russia introduces so many contradictions that we immediately reject it. And yet, we recognize that "comparative advantage" has already made our world what it is. It is a fact that sheep farming has, in two centuries, largely migrated to Australia and New Zealand. Manufacture of high-labor-content goods has migrated to Mexico and China. Production of aluminum has proceeded to Russia and other low-energy-cost countries. Financial services have grown disproportionably in the United States.

The most variable factor in world economic thinking today is population. Like global warming, militarism, religion, suburban sprawl, and other hope/fear worries, population growth arouses apprehension in some quarters. Schools of thought like the Club of Rome have come and gone, United Nations projections of future populations have waxed and waned. Sexual activity has been the source of population so far, and birth control has its fans, because it is argued that the world's resources won't support a decent life for a population substantially greater than we now have. My view is twofold: fecundity will decrease steadily in the future as even more people depart agricultural life and move to cities. As general prosperity increases with the absence of war, increased productivity, and birth control methods, the rapid population growth of the past century will diminish, and global stability of human organisms will be within reach. We still have a lot of wiggle room: the resources of the world can support on a sustained basis, an unknown higher number of people. There are thinkers who believe we are at the limit now, but I am not among that group.

Class is a more explosive topic than race. Economic advantage is attached to the name "class". One can speak of the "masses" and the "classes" in terms of revolution and re-distribution of capital. Those of long enough memory speak of how the working class stuck up for its rights, or how the peasant class persisted. There are always media reports of the privileges and excesses of the "upper class". I cannot stop people from indulging in these usages. There is no doubt that in the past, individual humans were consigned to certain occupations and positions in society, constituting "class", for generations upon generations. I get nervous when I read about those classes who in effect are asking larger society to confirm and perpetuate their membership in that class. I don't doubt that the farmers of Chiapas are perversely (in my view) banding together to demand that they be preserved as a class. I simply feel that such attempts to preserve classes are doomed by the successful decision of many participants to leave.

The United States prides itself on having a census every ten years. The Constitution says it must. The intention of this provision by our Founders was to provide Government with facts about our citizenry which would permit more practical decisions about many matters. From its beginning, census questions concerned the races, ages, and sexes of the respondents. Over the years, more commercial questioning crept into it: how many cars or telephones were in the household, for example. The attempt to answer questions about race is now more embarrassing than of practical import. The leading factor in this embarrassment is the heavy advent of persons of Hispanic language background, who cannot fairly answer questions about race in the context that they were originally designed.

CELEBRITIES

Who is not fond of celebrities? Certainly I have rarely met a person who is not. Most people I have known are anxious to gossip about actors, politicians, artists, sports figures or business personalities whose name and purposes have become well known. It matters little how these persons have become celebrities; the fact is that they are viewed and treated as such. I can't help being aware of them, and I have met a few. For the purpose of a book about the reality of internationalism, their celebrity status is closely associated now with the general world economy. Their Public Relations position is vital, and there is a world-wide industry ready to put additional spins on already well-known personal brands.

In studying the operations of the United Nations and its many agencies, for example, it is obvious that appeal to celebrities is an important component in raising money to support necessary activities. If you take a look at UNICEF, which uses famous figures from sports and entertainment, you find that immense sums are raised using the endorsement of those figures. Concert extravaganzas and rock music tours with big name recording artists are almost more successful than raising taxes, and this transcends national borders; very few countries are immune to the popularity of well-promoted or accidental fame. A full page advertisement in London's *Financial Times* shows a huge picture of Martina Hingis and Jacques Villeneuve, two major sports figures of the times, and announces that they are supporting the United Nations

Development Programme, headquartered in Geneva, whose objective is to halve world poverty by 2015. This advertisement solicits individual participation in the program, using the lure of celebrity participation, much as UNICEF has successfully done.

Long ago, the fame of monarchs and military heroes was so great that their names were assigned to historical periods, e.g., Ming Dynasty, Victorianism, the Napoleonic era. Fame, glory, and reputation have been ever-present factors for humanity. But not until recently has media attention, often paid-for in advance, developed such a concentration of private heroes for public tasting. Celebrities, whether self-promoted or exalted by others, are a real force. Organizations with international aspirations should make sure that they have lots of sports, entertainment, and intellectual celebrities associated with their causes.

Noteworthy is the huge growth of trans-national advertising and public relations firms. They serve the need for specific promotional work for growing commercial enterprises entering new countries and markets. They are also closely tied to name recognition and brand promotion crossing former boundaries of language, custom, and race. This activity is perhaps more important to the development of international stability than many more staid programs of governments and their related international agencies. Nor is public relations restricted to commercial topics. Governments, whether obscure or famous, employ specialists from this field to advance their viewpoint with the public and with other governments.

Promotion of destination tourism is closely related to celebrity presence and involvement. Las Vegas, Nevada, is a clear case. That city, with the fastest-growing population in the United States, is built on glamour even more than the old Hollywood was, and has a world-wide appeal to masses of ordinary folks all over the planet. It is not a conventional city like New York, London, or Rome, where generations of commerce and ideas have seeded huge entertainment arrangements. No, Las Vegas is a spacious playpen for the world. Its casinos, shows, restaurants, architecture and theme history is a fake in historical terms. But what a fake! Latest figures show that more than 40,000,000 visitors go there every year. This puts it far ahead of religious pilgrimages. Not only that, but Orlando, Anaheim, and their spectacular gambling-free theme parks are in second place for visitors in the United States. We were chastened when touring New Zealand a few years ago, to find that very few people could place our home city of Philadelphia, of which we are patriotic supporters. To our dismay, we found that most ordinary New Zealanders had just vaguely heard of it. However, they had a clear vision of Disney Land in California. To these people, Disney Land *was* the States.

It is hard for politicians and business leaders to become celebrities. They have to work too hard for too many years, and establish complex private networks of influence as they build their careers, and in many cases this takes the life out of them, literally and figuratively. Occasionally a Bill Gates, Warren Buffett, or George Soros will make the celebrity list, but more commonly it is a sports or entertainment figure. This is not to denigrate the hard work that a football hero or TV personality exerts. It is simply to state the obvious, that steady media coverage, particularly with TV, is a far more potent personal brand builder than that provided by years of plodding private work in business or even politics. Further, public entertainment, which is closely linked to celebrities, has economic and social implications for the world.

Adding emphasis to branding of products and persons, cities, regions and countries are in the process of putting a price tag on their names, too. At first this seems bizarre, but city councils in New York and Philadelphia are not alone in talking with legal specialists to see if they can appropriate the use of their own name, and monetize its value by selling the right to use it to others. And how could they not come to this conclusion? After all, for decades, the "naming rights" for many civic stadiums have been sold by governments to the high bidders in the commercial world. And where did this trick come from? Obviously, from the practice of naming a dormitory or gymnasium at a university in honor of the donor. And where did that idea come from? Donations made by the wealthy to the Church in ages past. In the Christian West, at least, it was common to put the name of the donor (Pope, King or Financier) in prominence on the building, even though austere custom often assigned a Saint's name to the building of a church.

Thus we establish celebrities, in the United States slipping so far as to name memorial interchanges on highways. Thus it has always been, but for the first time, those celebrities can have international appeal, and this is the reason I extend this reasoning: heavy financing and serious purpose can create international celebrities who set the agenda more pungently than the ideology of religions or philosophies of the past. The Princess Diana of the 20th Century surpasses the monarchial presumptions of the British Empire. The personality of Donald Rumsfeld exceeds the harsh reality of a "Shock and Awe" bombing campaign. Osama Ben Laden is a far more potent power on the strength of his reputation, dead or alive, than his handful of followers with their hi-jacked airplanes and suicide attacks.

The United States has led the world, if you care to look at it this way, in the establishment of these new worldwide celebrities; if we accept the reality that they and their associated personalities are at the heart of much of what really happens in the world, we must wonder if other centers of celebrity creation will arise. That is problematic. The World's largest population, China, has an established prejudice against celebrities. Interestingly, however, the Dalai Lama of Tibet, operating from India, has enormous celebrity status, as did Mahatma Gandhi. The Pope has celebrity in western circles, but not much in the East.

To be rich is not necessarily to be a celebrity. Many rich persons throughout the world seek to avoid that status, on the basis that it is a nuisance, or even that they might be targets of criminal activity. Philadelphia has its share of wealthy people, some of whom live in a style unknown to ordinary citizens, but mostly their fame is parochial, and even the wealthiest can walk the street without general recognition.

There is more of a celebrity factor involved in the life of a major international capital such as New York or London, and this also involves the wealthy who congregate in such places from the provinces. It is hard to say where these folks really live, and some years ago the appellation "Jet Set" was coined to suggest that they are always on the run, evading or encouraging the paparazzi as they make their way from Mediterranean to Caribbean gathering places. Only the tax man, it would seem, knows where they really live.

A twinge of envy enters my mind when I contemplate the life of a member of the jet set who does not fret over the price of a Beverly Hills mansion. It would be nice to travel as Queen Elizabeth does, and indicate with a nod of the head what luxury is desired. But there is a positive social contribution made by the rich, even if it is the last thing in their minds. Think about the value that a rich and/or celebrated person confers on the community! It is a seldom-considered matter. Some say that the rich provide and absorb shocking amounts of gross national income. (Translated: they make too much money). Some say the rich pay too little in taxes. I maintain that the presence of personal wealth, properly understood, plays a major part in the development of nations' prosperity, because its presence attracts more wealth, and the network of reciprocal wealth creates the big pools of liquid capital which sustain great civilizations. I am nervous in talking about such a subject. It seems so un-democratic, so snobby, so complacent. Yet I content myself with just that small twinge of envy, and am willing to be close to people with good resources. If pressed, I cite the empires of Greece, Rome, Egypt, Mexico, Persia to demonstrate that civilization goes with wealth and vice versa.

When it comes to actual dollars, pounds, euros, and yen, governments are delighted to identify wealth, because then it can be taxed. A social complainant may moan about the high compensation paid to athletes, movie stars, and officers of big corporations. The tax man, by contrast, rubs his hands . . . to a degree . . . when he reads about high salaries. More wages=more taxes! However, governments have learned, or should have, that it is not wise to over-tax the rich. The rich have infinite ways of hiding their assets, moving them to havens, and employing agents and servants to make sure that their wealth, though taxed, does not dissipate. Again referring to the Jet Set, it is the unannounced policy of wise governments to make sure that a hospitable welcome is advanced to those from outside jurisdictions. Particularly in a place like London, where Saudi princes, Indian maharajas, and Australian mining barons rub elbows, it is good for business not to be too rigorous in arguing about residency. If the British authorities make taxes too tough on outsiders, the visitors will simply fade away, and congregate in more congenial regimes. The merchants of London, New York, and similar venues depend on these wealthy patrons for their own living. A chill came over the New York scene, for example, when Mr. Koslowski chairman of Tyco Industries, illegally diverted shipment of some fine art he had purchased to a fraudulent address outside of the City, in order to avoid millions of dollars in sales tax. His action was criminal, and not to be approved. However, his was a showpiece prosecution. The authorities do not wish to initiate a vast pattern of going after these evaders. They only choose the most egregious cases, because they want New York to be seen as a "good" place for a rich person to perch.

If I seem overly cheerful about the rich and famous, and perhaps under-appreciative of the poor and needy, I defend myself by declaring that all of social life—seen through the prism of the centuries—is a zero sum game, in which there is a broad distribution and stirring of capital and fame. Few indeed are the families or individuals who create either one through more than two or three generations. World society grows and prospers through it all while some go up and some go down. Nor is it just the tax collector or early termination of life which determines the fortunes of the ages. There seems to be a built-in limit against excessive fame or fortune. The "might-have-beens" of each life are just that.

EXPATRIATION

Most ancestors of present-day North Americans came to this hemisphere in boats, and as children we learned about Columbus, the Puritans, and the Statue of Liberty immigrants. But many people came on foot, through the Bering Strait area, when Alaska and Siberia were joined by land. When the new Museum of Anthropology opened in Mexico City, it was not only a spectacular piece of architecture, but it introduced me and many others to the facts of this early settlement by people who became the native originals of America. I was charmed by its exhibits showing the developing life of our people before Europeans and Africans arrived. For the first time, I began to think seriously about our collective origins.

As in so many other developments in my lifetime, the newest scientific information, in this case archeological, quickly raised more questions than answers. The wide-ranging work of archeologists, ethnologists, and anthropologists, which has a long and honorable history, has stepped up to meet the public fascination. In Egypt, Greece, China, Mexico, and Africa there is no end to the digging and investigating. New revelations about human history emerge every week. There is now, also, an awesome ability to date the origin of artifacts, and DNA evidence about the biological descent of people.

We now have "a" picture of the evolution of humanity, and a notion of cultural development which is revealing, even if still incomplete. I am satisfied, more than I might have been 50 years ago, that the main lines of humanity's evolution are known. The great differences in cultures are understood and appreciated. Some have flourished, others have languished or disappeared. We are currently confronted with an intermingling of cultures which seems unprecedented, but in fact the record shows that human history has been one long story of movement and change. It's nothing new.

I am changing in front of my own self, to become a different being than my parents and grandparents, and I am heavily influenced by other cultures. I assume that the other hundreds of millions who are out there are changing, too. I expect my children to be vastly changed from me; this sometimes makes me existentially nervous, but it's a fact. It happens that I have not fathered children with a mother of another culture than my own. But that could easily have turned out differently. For many of our present U.S. population, including members of my own family, marriage outside the group is a frequent occurrence.

Aside from the mass movements of populations which have occurred in the past, and are still happening to a degree, there is always the movement of individual persons from place to place. In the recent past, migrations by individual decision making largely involved persons moving from Europe to the western hemisphere. In modern life, there has grown up a more complex arrangement in which people are moving in all directions on all continents, providing stimulating cross currents in pre-existing cultures . . . and sometimes stress for all concerned. I welcome this development, which increases the interconnection between all peoples and cultures. The personal adjustments which result from the movement are sometimes awkward, and result in unforeseen outcomes, but they are enriching to civilization.

Many U.S. families can testify to the mixture of cultures which has occurred in the past 200 or 300 years (a brief period in historical terms), and I cite some examples to illustrate some of the current occurrences which have an influence in how the larger world decides to deal with the steady increase in intermingling.

Just now, my friend Eric Biddle sent me a newspaper clipping relating that the Canadian government, in a statement under the aegis of Queen Elizabeth as head of state, declared that injustices had been committed against the Acadians beginning in 1755. That was the event immortalized by Longfellow in his poem "Evangeline", when ancestors of mine were ousted from Nova Scotia and came to Philadelphia. My mother, born in Montreal, lived 3/4 of her 95 years in the States, only 500 miles from her origins, but in a psychological sense I think she never left Canada. Am I a Canadian?

My friend Angeles Stiteler left Mexico as a result of her mother's marriage to a professor who had a job in the States. She later became an American citizen, and has been living in the U.S. for 60 years. She says she is still dealing with dual personality and dual citizenship. Mexico has made it possible for former citizens who have moved away, to vote in Mexican federal elections. Her children and grandchildren are sometimes identified as being of "Hispanic" descent, although her grandchildren are less than ¼ Mexican.

Without completely addressing the question of United States citizenship laws, the Mexican government has recently, through its network of consulates, begun issuing personal identification documents, including photos, to Mexican nationals who reside in the United States. Those officials and many U.S. local and business officials, encourage the acceptance of these identifications in the absence of other papers. The argument is advanced that it is better to have someone identified, rather than have him or her unidentified.

A Canadian cousin married a German, and her descendents are living in Bavaria today. Another cousin married a Chinese, and a son of that marriage comes from Hong Kong to visit. Still another married a Vietnamese, with numerous offspring still resulting. Who are they?

I traveled to Japan to visit a cousin, Scott Drayer, who in the fortunes of young life, became an expatriate resident of that country. He lives in the provincial Japanese capital of Kanazawa, is a gregarious, capable, bi-lingual person. He owns property, is paid a salary by a Japanese university. He is an income tax payer to both the Japanese and U.S. authorities under rules promulgated by the two countries. From Japan's point of view he is a permanent resident, and is building up credits under the Japanese pension system. He has disputes over real estate and other legal matters in which he feels his foreign-ness is a handicap, but he is developing a Japanese life which is difficult but productive.

I don't have a solution for these individual and collective problems, all of which inhibit movement across national borders. Most people are content, and wish to stay where they are. Even inside the United States, with its ever-beckoning green pastures and mighty movements into formerly sparsely-settled areas, the distribution of population changes fairly slowly.

So what? Why should I be conscious of these historical anomalies, which merely prove that the world's population continues to mix and change as the ages unfold. Why should I worry if a relatively small number of people have to endure bureaucracy, even injustice, because of the fact of their own dislocation from their own "group"?

The reason for my interest is my conclusion that generations ahead will see the need to create new legal and practical clothing for a growing class of persons who do not regard themselves as irrevocably bound to the paradigms of a particular citizenship, religion, political adherence or race. There is muted but real protest now, within the U.S., about attempts to classify persons by ethnic and linguistic affiliation. Privacy laws are in place to prevent unwanted disclosure of personal opinions and confidential information. But as I write this, attempts are being made, so far unsuccessfully, to draft a "European" constitution, which is to define for the several hundreds of millions living in that area of the world, just what "European-ness" signifies. Other countries (Iraq is a good example) have serious problems in defining just what makes a person a citizen. Even harder are the cases where a country has different classes of citizen.

I do not have sympathy for those who would deny responsibility of citizenship, or those who feel that the least possible government or public identification of a citizen by authorities is the best condition for humanity. That is an extreme version of Libertarian political opinion. No, my view is that each person, beginning from childhood, should embrace a feeling of contribution to the public welfare. Ancient religious practice commands a tithe to that public welfare, and it is a worthy command. My concern and sometimes complaint is that nations do not make it easy for their citizens to move about in an unhindered way. I would speak up for international citizenship, or renunciation of national citizenship except that such a course of action seems premature until the general practices of security, legality and identification become more evenly applied throughout the world.

In the perceived triumph of world capitalism, it is ironic that corporate activity is essentially fungible. The actions of companies, wherever they occur, are valid and binding on their employees, customers and suppliers. Corporate networks and ownership transcend the borders of nations, and we have invented new words like "trans-national" to describe their activities. Corporations or limited-liability business arrangements are granted immortality and universality, while the ordinary human has neither quality. The human rights extended by governments to individual Czechs, Pakistanis or Chinese are still greatly divergent.

Several years ago, I studied ABB Corporation's structure. It is a large world-scale operation with business interests in most countries—either sales or production. It had over 1200 separate subsidiaries which had been established over the 100+ years of its existence. Such businesses invariably have the finest specialists that money can buy to make sure that their human and financial resources can be universally available for a price. That means that where borders need to be crossed by either people, goods and services, or by money, they have the skill and knowledge to do it.

Taxes, tariffs, passports, contracts and all the paraphernalia of commerce are vital to world trade, and hence to the livelihoods of all people. It is not an accident that trans-national firms like IBM, Siemens, or Sony are not even described any longer as "American", "German" or "Japanese". Even if a left-over opinion exists, it is in the process of being leveled out, because the fact is that no country controls these firms. Theoretically, their stockholders control them, but that is debatable, because usually management controls things, and management invariably consists of legions of persons of different civil nationality. I extend this interpretation only to show the startling difference between how the world treats business corporations and how it treats citizens.

Traditionally, citizens of a given nation were expected to be protected by their own governments, even beyond their borders. Several generations ago, when travel by citizens was considered a privilege of upper class moneyed persons, letters were created from government officials, asking their counterparts in other governments to extend courtesy and protection to the traveler. These ad hoc arrangements later were made routine throughout the world in the growth of the passport system. The fine print on my U.S. passport, for example, reads: "The Secretary of State of the United States of America hereby requests all whom it may concern to permit the citizen/national of the United States named herein to pass without delay or hindrance and in case of need to give all lawful aid and protection."

Whose laws? Whose protection? This is always a big problem, and leads to treaties about extradition, for example. Often there are high-profile criminal cases. (Ira Einhorn, the Philadelphia trunk murderer who hid out for many years in Europe and is now encased in a U.S. prison, is a good example.) The public is always fascinated by the emotional distress of a U.S. person detained in a foreign jail or courtroom. And newspapers in countries like Mexico eagerly report the happenings when their citizens get caught up in the U.S. justice system. Another quirk is that many countries punish their own citizens if they violate regulations about leaving their own country to visit another country without complying with intricate regulations. Recent newspaper accounts report prosecution being pursued by the United States against travelers who violated the embargo on Cuban travel six or seven years ago. In Japan during the period of 200 years before the "opening" of the country in the mid 19th century, persons who left Japan and later returned were simply executed.

The practice of asking a country in advance if it is permissible for a citizen of another nation to enter that country legally, is covered under the umbrella of "visas". These are instructions to low-level border control people from higher officials to permit entry under prescribed conditions. In many circumstances, a visa is not required. For example, I visited Japan without prior notice; I showed up at the Tokyo airport with a passport only, because I knew that the Japanese routinely admit persons traveling on U.S. passports without visas. The United States, by contrast, requires visas for visitors from most countries.

Many aspects of international travel are ludicrously old-fashioned hand-me-downs of an earlier day. Customs duties on merchandise are frequently found. Regulations about carrying cash are published, most of which are unenforceable without a physical search of the traveler's body. A lot of this stuff is ridiculous and complicating for the average traveler, and is kept on the books mostly out of habit, and to confront border crossers with a reminder of the power of "the authorities" to detain them if they need a pretext.

I cannot emphasize too heavily that it is easier for a corporation to move $100 million dollars by wire from Philadelphia to Toronto, than for a private citizen to put a television set in the back seat of his car and try and get it and his body across the border at Niagara Falls. I hope I live to see the day when border crossing is as easy as using the bridge to go from Philadelphia to Camden. I regret that the current trend works against the individual unless he or she is part of a larger and presumably more controllable group.

COMMUNICATION

Aside from mutes who don't have any choice, we start communicating with each other from the cradle. Life itself seems to be unending communication from there to the grave. It is obvious that person-to-person passing of sound, visual information, and data sets the stage for all world activity, but there has been so much hyperbole about communication in the past decade that many of us have lost track of the basics, confused by the marketing programs of "high technology".

Let's talk first about the languages of mankind. Fascinating as they are, and difficult as they are to master for those not born to them, they are the crystallization of thought for all humans, and in audible form, they fill the need for verbal intercourse. Experts continue to make great progress in the ancient goal of complete inter-translatability of tongues. Computing power has made it feasible to do this electronically, so that intelligent language sounds can already be converted into other sounds with good accuracy. With reasonable scientific progress in the next generation, I expect that this problem will be solved. Casual travelers and diplomats will be relieved of their inability to speak on a one-on-one basis to someone of different language origins. Just as huge computers have solved the complexities of chess, so will the complexities of language be mastered.

The solution to oral translation among the languages of earth is necessary, and is probably close at hand. However, the idea of a universal language which would become the world's major choice for communication has already progressed through the advance of the English language. The need for translatability on a planetary level is made somewhat less pressing because of the adoption of English as a required skill among those participating in commerce, science, and education. Increasingly this practical usefulness extends to ordinary people as well.

I am continuously surprised to observe the infinite numbers of ways in which the English tongue has filled a need. For example, I was amused to meet an Israeli traveler at the French castle of Fontainbleau, who complained that the authorities there had not provided directional signs in English. He said that as a person who traveled widely, he expected English-language materials to be available.

Without prejudice against all other languages, it would probably be convenient, and helpful to the further development of world relationships, if English continues to prevail as an international standard. Airline pilots, financial institutions, security personnel and scientists need a common spoken and written language on an hour-by-hour basis, even if the vast majority of folks with localized needs continue to use less generally known tongues.

The evolution of speech led finally to the development of writing, which permitted communication without the bodily presence of another individual. Eventually, reproduction in writing, by hand copying and then printing, magnified this ability, and led to a vast growth of indirect, impersonal communication. The nineteenth century brought modern newspapers to the entire world, with high-speed presses and vast distribution networks.

Now newspapers (to which I am perhaps unhealthily addicted) represent just one of many public communication options which are available to those with the capacity to pay for them. The Scott household subscribes to cable television, and has individual desk-top computers on-line. Telephones bring us London or Tokyo on demand. And if we really want to be slow and backward, we rely on FAX machines, the United States Mail, and commercial shipping services like United Parcel Service for overnight delivery of bulky materials. I classify our household as technologically up-to-date, not at the outer edge of technology, but within modern boundaries. We spend more money than most of mankind in our search for fast communication, but my guess is that the world will quickly surpass our level of technology in the next generation. Cell phones are being sold throughout the world at the level of around 500,000,000 units per year. Even allowing for loss, replacement of older sets with new, and with improving spectrum arrangements, this is a staggering figure. It indicates that the world's 6,000,000,000 inhabitants shortly will be in touch with their peers everywhere, electronically. Observation of the phone habits of residents of Tokyo or Sao Paulo will confirm that this is so. The U.S. has such extensive wired connections that land lines are still the preferred technique here. In most of the developing world, wireless is storming ahead in market penetration. For voice communication, there is no doubt in my mind that the cost and prevalence of wireless audio communication will result in very cheap and very good service within ten years, for all of mankind. The only remaining barrier to one-on-one communication will be that of language, and voice-recognition techniques will shortly solve most of that problem.

Audio communication, from its initiation by Alexander Graham Bell, has always been a thoroughly human activity. Among possible activities it has never seemed bizarre or aberrant. It is not hard to learn, it can be manipulated by young and old, woman and man, large and small. I have never heard a criticism that telephony encourages vice, degrades morals, or induces passive psychology. I have visited an Amish family in Pennsylvania which maintains its telephone outside the boundaries of its farm property, so as not to introduce a forbidden mechanism into its house. Amusingly, the family uses the phone, but departs its owned property to do so. But that is a rare situation. The generality of mankind today looks on phones as a vital piece of infrastructure, in the same league as the availability of electrical power from the grid. And they are willing to carry a cell phone in their purse or on their belt to emphasize the importance of their need in this respect.

Bell's simple request, "Please come here, Mr. Watson, I need you", uttered 125 years ago in a laboratory, became the precursor of tens of trillions of phone calls, which are essentially personal contacts one-on-one, assisted by engineered mechanisms which permit accomplishment of this human need over infinite distances. It is essential to understand that this phenomenon is *person-to-person* with all the psychological involvements of actual speech, plus some added features, of which the principal one is that you cannot physically touch the other person, either to kiss or to kill. Less important, you cannot see the other person, although that omission is being taken care of, like the language problem. A telephone conversation is symmetrical, like a face-to face meeting. That is to say, equal engineering weight is given to the receiver and the sender. Equal capacity is allocated to each participant because it is unknown in advance just how much time and effort will be taken by each in either listening or speaking. Therefore, plenty of extra capacity must be provided so that each party has unlimited ability to respond to the other.

Transmission of electrical impulses by a conducting wire was the initial method of making a telephone work, and that type of transmission is still the backbone of the world's telephone network. Soon after its invention, however, inventors came up with ways to transmit these impulses through air, and radio was born. Then came instantaneous personal messages by radiophone, which merely represented a change in the method of signal transmission. The world was now ready to communicate around the globe, still on a single-message person-to-person basis. There didn't necessarily have to be a conducting wire. Marconi proved in 1901 that you could throw a signal from Newfoundland across the Atlantic to Ireland without a cable. The rest of the 20th century was composed of improvements in technique, culminating in the development of cell phones in the last part of the century.

A major transmission technology recently arrived on the scene. It vastly increased the speed, accuracy and economic cost of communications in general. That was the idea of turning speech into streams of photons (light particles), instead of the electromagnetic waves which were used in both wired and wireless applications. This improvement did not alter the social requirements for person-to-person speech, but it cheapened the cost immensely, thereby preserving cable communication (as distinct from wireless), as a realistic long-range option.

Audio communications by their nature are extensions of the human voice, and therefore symmetrical, or "one-on-one". Most other methods of communication are asymmetrical. Mass communication modes (television, newspapers, films, recorded music and the like) rely on the creation of a package of information which is to be distributed to thousands and millions of people, but there is little or no capacity for direct feed-back from the receivers of the information.

I now return to more primitive modes of communication, which I will skip over in synopsis, although we continuously return to them in sophisticated and unsophisticated ways. Writing on surfaces and then carrying those surfaces to a distance for delivery to a particular person is the most obvious. Now we use paper, and we call it "mail". Egyptian princesses probably used papyrus, and mediaeval monks had vellum. The transaction is again symmetrical, in that a response may be expected, and therefore if there is an outgoing Pony Express, there must be a return trip. It is true that a written message is less personal than a conversation, and its contents can be seen by others, or easily copied. Nonetheless, it is basically a one-to-one conveyance.

Early in the development of civilization the idea of asymmetrical communication arose. The notion probably started with clay tablets, then scrolls, and finally books. These were intended from the outset to be the composition of an individual, aimed at a larger audience, and without necessarily contemplating any direct response requiring the provision of engineering capacity to handle it.

For many centuries, symmetrical and asymmetrical communication co-existed without evaluation, each filling a human need, with relatively small social cost. As time passed, permanent asymmetrical work began to accumulate. Libraries, storage of ancestral records, and the output of religious art and culture became the fabric of nations. Although most communication had disappeared into dust or thin air, permanent works started to pile up. The social cost built up, too: the cost to society of creating and maintaining written, printed, filmed, or magnetic records became significant.

Movies on photographic film, first silent, then with audio accompaniment became a major force for communication, and in parallel, the phonograph enabled one person's work of music to be duplicated so that millions could listen to the same song. Soon television was to complete the work of concentrating talent in selected locations, and then duplicating images and sounds for distribution to the world's millions. In the process, this distribution became the pre-occupation of publicists or of governments, and the bane of many observers of the situation. Much commentary was created in the last half of the 20th century decrying the centralization of the media. Everyone wanted to be that movie producer, or network impresario. But we, the world's 6 billion, became the absorbers of mass communication created not by one person, but by a process employing perhaps hundreds of thousands. The meaning of this for the development of civilization is unclear. It is clear, however, that the public's preference for this style of civilization remains high. Tastes for printed media versus electronic media vary from time to time, but the evidence is that the public throughout the world is willing, even eager, to consume communication which is essentially centralized and controlled by a few.

Some feel that this centralization is a near monopoly, and hence dangerous to public welfare. My feeling is that the centralization will self-destruct. The proliferation of media outlets and specialization of talent and topics is the main reason, but also there is a growing demand for particular information from consumers. If so the ratio of producers to consumers might change substantially.

Even so, it must be admitted that mass distribution in the media still favors the asymmetrical mode. By any measure, this distribution is passive, in the sense that there is no provision for back-communication. Occasionally, one will see cartoons involving a viewer throwing something at his TV screen by way of response, but this is the exception. It looks to me as though mass one-way communication will further dominate the developing world, until the sophistication comes about which results in diversity. Pico Iyer has written a humorous book, *Video Night in Katmandu,* which describes in gleeful detail the universal saturation of film and TV in bazaars and other old-fashioned venues in the world. It won't take many more years for the full panoply of mass communication to be available everywhere to all sectors of society.

The particular genius and stylishness of the Internet has to do with its essential trend toward one-on-one communication. The economics and engineering of the net, with modern broadband equipment (only now beginning to be widely available), permits a user to be connected at all times to a web of communication to which instantaneous response can be made. For example, if an audio or data message is received by an individual receiver at a computer station, the receiver can respond either immediately or at a later time, but with full ability in engineering terms to respond completely. If you send me an image, I can send you an equally complex image. If you send me text message, I can respond in equally complete language. While the installed engineering to permit this symmetrical response is only in it infancy, there seems little doubt that it will be the major non-military capital expense for civilization in the 21st century, and that by a hundred years from now, all individuals on the planet will, in actual practice, be able to communicate directly with all other individuals.

Admittedly, the direct one-on-one response permitted by the Internet is partially artificial in human psychological terms. If you order goods and services, you are probably dealing with an automated response at the other end. You may sense that you have ordered an airline ticket from a person, but your sense is false. There can be person-to-person communication, via e-mail or in postings to web pages. However, the important thing, whether actual communications are personal or automated, is that the network is in place which gives *everyone* in the world the theoretical ability to be in touch with everyone else directly.

The aggregate effect of decisions by people to take advantage of this opportunity or not to, is a subject for statisticians and systems engineers to ponder. This pondering is analogous to that which has been going on for the last hundred years about the sizing of electrical power grids, telecommunication networks, and water distribution systems. There are specialists who decide how many people are likely to turn on lights, start an electric furnace, or otherwise cause demand for electrical power from the electrical grid. Likewise, the major telephone companies throughout the world have voluminous resources to back up their judgment about the timing and patterns of human audio contacts. Water suppliers, though less global in character, have amazing data about when and where toilets are flushed or lawns sprinkled. The world has greatly benefited from surprisingly accurate plans and guesses about this kind of traffic.

The electrical, audio-communication and water grids referred to are mature in character; their requirements for engineering capital are well known, and can be extrapolated. The Internet is another matter. It is so new, and in its best dress still rather expensive, that its presence is novel, and its cost unknown. In that respect, it reminds me somewhat of the air travel industry, which to upper income U.S. persons is almost regarded as a public utility of a commodity nature. However, at the global level, air transport has barely made a dent in the travel habits of the six billion of us who live here, so that the eventual social cost of providing that transport for everyone is unknowable.

In Internet operations, due consideration must be given to traffic, and facilities provided which take account of that traffic. In the U.S., there has been a lull, which I believe is temporary, in the relationship between network capability, and usage. Too much capacity was added during previous years, and usage of that capacity did not meet the optimistic projections of the many participants.

There is little hard data which is available to me to confirm the opinion. AOL Time-Warner wrote off Internet capacity assets of nearly $100 billion in 2002. This tax and accounting action is a clear indication that serious asset over-building was occurring, but I regard that as a temporary pause. The Internet consists of computers, cable and wireless connections, and switching arrangements. It also consists of web pages and sites for the accumulation of astronomical amounts of data, which represents an immense storehouse of human capital. Only a small portion of this data may be accessed "free" by the using public. There is no way for me or anyone else to calculate its size, but there is a further immense storehouse which is available only to those who have the key. This storehouse is the cascading number of private networks which are used for specific purposes. Only those who belong and have paid a price can use the Internet to reach this data, and when hackers succeed in getting inside the magnetic fence, scandal and fraud is the result.

At an investment conference oriented toward the Internet and companies specializing in turning it into private profit, I heard the concerns of specialists considering its future. At present many of the assumptions and dreams surrounding this new medium may be exaggerated, but there are true believers who think that after a pause for consolidation the march toward an Internet world will resume. Among all the believers there is, however, concern that there are seeds of self-destruction contained within the present system. First is the possibility that ill-purposed individuals can disable all or parts of the system by conscious acts of hacking. Beyond that is a concern for privacy, which is a surrogate for civil rights worries which have been around for years. We deal with uninvited sales approaches at our front door. We deal with unsolicited phone calls. Both of these are personal, and we can respond. But the Internet is highly impersonal, and although it is partially symmetrical and we *can* respond, we are confronted by a feeling of powerlessness in our response. If we receive unwanted or undesirable contacts, we cannot retreat except by withdrawing completely. The sheer volume of incoming electronics, aimed at us not as individuals, but as statistics, is impossible to filter without a strong time commitment. The combination of purposeful individuals and powerful computers can track our habits and preferences to a painful and intrusive degree.

An important factor in Internet activity which is generational in impact is the question of magnetic storage of data. This study is of a different character than that of day-to-day operations. Instead of storing our intangible thoughts on stone, as our distant ancestors did, or on paper or transparent film, as more recently, we now aspire to use the magnetic materials associated with computers to store for tomorrow or for the ages the products of our minds. Our technical ability to store things forever now exceeds the amount of material we are capable of making a decision about keeping. When we have an empty bookshelf, we suspect that in future years we will ultimately fill it with volumes. In the same manner, we suspect that savable stuff will expand to fill our empty magnetic storage. The new element in this equation is that our magnetic storage capability is infinite for all practical purposes. (And if magnetic storage should prove finite, scientists are working hard to provide other, even more elegant storage methods.)

Startling developments have occurred in the 1:1 universe of individual communication. The world-wide telephone network, as true a leveling force as has ever been unleashed, mushroomed in the late 20th century, and permitted interactive response in unparalleled profusion. The economics favored cheap audio conversation, with burgeoning electronic techniques: optical circuitry, high and low frequency wireless circuits. Trans-oceanic message costs became so cheap that it paid to have English-speakers in India do telemarketing to United States consumers.

There is another major form of communication which does not involve direct audible or visual participation by a human body to create, transmit or receive communication. That domain is data communication, as distinct from audible or readable information. As mentioned previously, this is a major feature of the public Internet. However, it is also a major endeavor of private and public wholesale data transmission which arises mainly from the world's commercial and governmental activity. Banks, warehouses, military operations, and a thousand other activities generate data which is untouched by human hands either in the receipt or the dispatch.

The creation of data and its interchange is as old as mankind. However, in the 20th century, the accumulation and distribution of data by electro-technical means gathered great speed. Pure numbers began to be transmitted by telegraph in the 19th century in code, with the famous Morse code dominating, and these methods persisted until the mid 20th, when the ability to accumulate data in electro-magnetic form began to cascade. The earliest attempts by Edison and Johnson to make mass reproducible "records" of music and speech were really analogs between the frequencies and amplitudes of audible noise, and the mechanical grooves of the discs or wires which served to preserve these amplitudes and frequencies for later re-play. After some decades of development for these analogs, miniaturization of circuits and improvements in magnetic materials permitted the design of electromagnetic storage of immense amounts of whatever needed to be stored. Undreamed of quantities of data, once abandoned to the ages or stored on paper and other passive materials, were about to be stored.

An even more startling scientific development now accelerated the rudimentary storage methods of electrical pioneers, which had been largely analog in nature. This development was digitalization. The means was mathematical, and scientists deconstructed numerals, letters and other symbols, reducing them to an electrical code based on binary numbers. These coded data could readily be stored, be extracted from storage with ease, and transmitted a foot away or ten-thousand miles away, to waiting machinery which could de-code and return the data to a form immediately understandable to the human being receiving it. The magnetic discs in computers became the processors of most of mankind's data within one generation. Suddenly, the amount of data possessed by humanity became far larger than all the verbal, written or seen communications ever indulged in by human beings. This assertion rocks me, even as I make it, because it is such a major change for our thinking, and its realization underlies most of the changes which are vitally affecting our world economy and the way we work and communicate with one another. Suddenly, the ability to exchange data from one point to another challenges the personal contact of a book, newspaper, phone call, or TV program.

This advent of high-speed, high-capacity computers has been a key ingredient in all kinds of communication, both mass and individualistic. The Internet emerged as a system combining major features of both and its features are still being sorted out. However, the main intellectual development is solid and in place. That is, the new concept of globally pervasive, point-to-point contact between billions of actual human beings and actual sources of data is well started. Even the cost of such a titanic venture appears to be well within the ability of the world's economy to handle it.

In mass sales and advertising, those who are trying to induce others to indulge in commerce measure the number of eye contacts which their advertisements are likely to have. For example, a printed ad appearing in a magazine of known circulation, will have an estimated viewing which is studied both before and after its appearance. This is the work of advertising agencies, and its evaluation has much to do with why the Sunday paper is as thick with ads as it is. These ads are not "wasted", as critics say. It may be a pity that more trees are ground up to feed the printing presses of this world, but it is not true that no one sees or reads the ads. People do, and there are those who make a living out of measuring this response. Ditto for visual information conveyed by TV. Ditto for "word-of-mouth" contacts between people. Ditto for elections and opinion polls. There is an immense industry, very professional, of people who measure the amount and force of human contacts, either for personal gain or academic study. These persons are now busy at work to determine the human results of the Internet's existence. No doubt there are tomes beyond tomes which already detail the magnitude of this activity.

The notion of the individual human as a data center is intriguing, and provides a useful spiritual leveling process. I have earlier discounted scary visions of media masters who control the world's thought process from some central command post. As long as there are human beings, both creating data, receiving it, and storing some of it, there cannot be universal control. Each human can process only a limited amount of communication, and there are only 24 hours in a day.

The practical use of the Internet can be either active or passive; unlike books, movies, and TV, in which the user can only be passive, the Internet user can either generate or receive information. This distinction is crucial, because it introduces the notion that any one person can be in direct touch with another. Admittedly, the same was true two hundred years ago when mail became a practicality, or one hundred years ago when telephony began its influence. Now, the immediacy, technical universality, and storage possibilities of Internet data raises world interdependence to a previously undreamed-of capability. Users of the Internet may simply be enthralled by the possibility of cheap world-wide direct communication. Or they may be enthralled by the "library" function, in which the knowledge of the ages is, so to speak, at their fingertips.

Potentially, the use of the Internet as a political weapon by individuals is both frightening and heartening as it affects decency and order in general human affairs. It does not take much to imagine the contacts, opinions, plans and execution which can come into the competitive operations of groups, companies, nations, religious bodies, and the like. The opportunity to avoid structures and go right to the heart of things is tempting, and is being done. These contacts, and the hope and threat of them, are a source of concern to those who administer the great affairs of mankind as we know them. Therefore, the Internet may justly be viewed as a stronger revolutionary force, for good or ill, than say the Communist movement or the French Revolution.

Some attention to the technical character of the Internet is justified, but I think that the main concept will remain intact. At the technical level, the development of faster and more capable computers, with corresponding improvements in hardware and software quality, is sure to happen. It is also moderately interesting to consider the methods by which data is sent and received by the humans who are involved. There is a great commercial fight at the moment about the type of wireless or wired communication method which will prevail. I cannot predict the outcome of this debate, which may unfold in amazing configurations and appliances. I am inclined to the opinion that wireless methods will prevail over a very long period, but am mainly interested in the results of all this interaction. My hope is that personal contact and the interest that it infers, will result in a more mature, peaceful, productive and entertained world.

FINANCE

As you age, it is easy to get interested in money. When you are young, and usually need money, it is elusive and desirable. When you are old, and have seen the power of money for good and ill, it can prey on your mind with worries about 'will it last until the end?', or 'should I try to leave something for the next generation?' You may conclude that money can buy love or civil power; you may go so far as to feel that most human endeavors including the act of living or dying are measured in monetary terms. For an example, you may consult a poem by Robert Frost called "Provide, Provide". Its theme is the fate of a famous actress, reduced to being a cleaning lady in her old age. The final stanzas of the poem admonish the reader to remember that no memory of early stardom eases her pain at the end. The poet even implies that it is better to have a purchased friendship late in life than none at all.

Frost catches poignantly the feelings encountered by older folks both rich and poor, as they look back on lives of missed or taken opportunities. Many of them think too steadily about how they will be supported, or how their dependents will fare. It is true that the Bible counsels all humanity not to worry, but "consider the lilies of the field. They toil not, neither do they spin". However, in his poem, Frost squarely faces the need for financial resources in old age.

I make this reminder about money in the private world in order to lead up to remarks about public finance. This book is a discussion of things that make the world tick, and public finance is one of the most significant of those things: in the same league as public health and the formation of families. At the personal or family level, money is the most commonplace topic for all persons. It causes family fights, and establishes powerful figures in business. Its possession seems to us an act of chance. If we inherit it, we soon forget those who accumulated it. If we make it, whether in salaries or gain, we get used to it as a right bestowed on us by history. Or, to put forward the classic Trade Union argument in labor negotiations: "Once a benefit is secured, it must never be given back". To put it bluntly, money is the gold standard of human understanding.

Still, the discussion of money in families, though it is a universal theme, should not be mentioned without acknowledging that for very many humans, there is almost nothing in the way of either capital or income. A Bangladeshi woman's entire capital may be a gold bracelet. A Mexican farmer might have a cow. I am speaking from an elevated personal situation in which I have been careful about money. I started out life with some in hand, and with good fortune I still have both capital and income. Therefore, my outlook and advice is prejudiced indeed, because the majority of humanity has little of either.

I wish for personal prosperity for all, but I understand that this is for the indefinite future. I am interested in money and finance at the private level, and I advise others to act with studied prudence. However, private financial virtue is not the main thrust of this book. Instead I turn to the public arena, where there is much to see and learn.

The mechanical flow of money through the global economy is now well documented and it has vast unseen consequences for individuals. This documentation and refinement of systems of exchange of value has accelerated. The doing of it has been necessary to accommodate global transactions, for the new science of manipulating economies, and for the description of both capital and income as measurable entities. The computer and the communication system are indispensable instruments for this as part of the studies of economics which have proliferated in the past 200 years. These studies have opened the eyes of kings and presidents. I often think of the naïve view of the old emperor of China, who understood that if you just successfully taxed each Chinese a penny a year, you would have an immense treasury at your disposal. But this emperor, and his contemporaries, did not have a sophisticated understanding of money and its infinite possibilities. The so called 'dismal science' of economics had not yet arisen.

The 191 nations of the world now have measuring devices available to them which offer an increasingly sharp vision of what is going on in their own economies. Further, they share much of this data with the world community, both private and public. Economic statistics now form the basis of world economic order. The formation and recent development of the European Union is the most perfect case for present study. A generation of trained economists and politicians were faced with creating a completely new, modern economic arrangement, which depended for its very existence on economics . . . not language, not religion, not race . . . but numbers.

A generation ago, there was much more skepticism about the numbers that any financial arm of a government displayed. There was mistrust about tax avoidance, overseas hiding of money, devious corporate bookkeeping and accounting standards which varied from place to place. By no means have all of these problems been solved, but mid and high-level bureaucrats of the nations have now been highly trained, in many cases at the best North American and European universities. There is a growing international caste of practitioners who understand the benefit to themselves and their nations of getting a real grasp of economic measurements. The president of the Federal Reserve Bank of St. Louis, in a recent speech, emphasized that in the United States practically all of the economic data which is accumulated is available to the public, to stock markets, to the government at the same time. He said that there are few if any financial secrets. Specifically, he said, when the Federal Open Market Committee sets interest rates, always a subject of intense scrutiny, those who make the decision are working with the same economic measurements available to economists world-wide at the same time.

Not all the news is good when you are capable of measuring such things: inflation data, bank reserves, government budgets and actualities, domestic and international borrowing . . . just to name a few. Governments, banks, and corporations are just as nervous as anyone else about releasing "bad" news which causes them or their friends distress and problems. Even "good" news can be worrisome, and there is a good deal of background discussion among the experts as to just how much information should be released, and to whom. Officials are always worried about financial speculators, and potential unfriendly forces. In the same way that a particular company can see its stock price hit or boosted by the release of unusual statistics, so there is diffidence in high places about the "spin" that is put on data.

In current times, the most fascinating aspect of the increasingly trustworthy financial data is the case of the European Union. Here, the nations of that group, in addition to supporting a unified currency, the Euro, are bound by treaty to undertake certain actions on the basis of budget deficits which are themselves required to be within prescribed limits. Only if there is general feeling that each of the nations is presenting valid measurements can such a scheme even get started. Much emphasis is put on the rate of inflation or deflation of prices for goods and services, and these data are worked into treaty arrangements and studied by a cadre of experts.

There are skeptics who believe that no promises to balance budgets or stabilize prices can keep together formerly separate countries which are trying to integrate themselves. These skeptics argue that eventually the nations involved will split apart and go their own way. Nonetheless, the existence of measurable data is a distinctive change for the world. It has come about through the huge increase in international transactions, involving the banking industry and its access to modern computers and communication.

The ability to move financial obligations by wire is alone a mammoth improvement over the old days when money was moved by courier.

In another sector, essentially all the nations of the world . . . rich, poor, populous or not . . . are members of the International Monetary Fund, with contractual rights to borrow, temporarily, various other currencies, based on IMF's information about internal banking conditions in those nations. Despite occasional charging against police barricades by opponents of "globalism", the need for this international arrangement has remained strong. It is supported by practically every government, no matter what the internal politics of a given nation may be at the moment. Inevitably, IMF, which charges fees to maintain this system, has to levy its charges upon its subscribers, and it imposes requirements about the use of the funds provided. All of this depends, yet again, on the accuracy of the information which is provided. It augurs well for the stability of the world financial structure that defaults, mis-information or fraud have been rare in this vital sub-structure of the world system. Even the arguments about the financial structure of the defeated and collapsed regime in Iraq reveal that there are well understood data about capital, monetary values, production output, outstanding loans and all the other facets of modern economic life. This data is in the hands of both insiders and outsiders, and can be reconstructed if mislaid. The most hermit kingdom of the planet, North Korea, has financial data which is well understood by outside experts.

Most individuals who understand their own finances believe that they should make more income instead of less, should save more than is spent, and should have some plan about future resources. It is reasonable that if they think at all about public finance, they should also take the view that governments should raise more and more money, should have balanced "budgets", and should have a long-term view of how things are likely to go in the public "future". After all, citizens have been reading about five-year plans (originally popularized by the Russian communists), and there are regular pontifications in the media about pension plans that fail, social security funding which might run out in 20 years, balance-of-trade statistics and other such information which, if it existed at all in my youth was the province of specialists and not talked about in public. As a result of all this, the public at large in modern, organized countries, has a rough idea of what is going on in the world flow of public capital. This was *not* formerly the case.

However, the creation and maintenance of money and credit is still a somewhat mysterious function of government. Controlling the currency is still perceived as a sovereign function of nations, particularly sensitive to nationalistic politics. The conditions of public and private credit are usually dictated by professional bankers and economists, although one set of professionals may find its control challenged by another set. When kings and queens used to rule by divine right, they had a vested interest in having their citizens believe that monarchy was inspired by heaven, and public finance was a protected zone of high privilege and inside information. Public money and credit is now coordinated by corps of specialists. Control of it is probably a more prized aspect of governance than command of armies or religions. In effect, its controllers have become the monarchs of the day.

In early centuries, governments were constrained by money considerations, and there were then, as now, only three ways to get money into a public treasury: taxation, conquest, or borrowing. Before the advent of paper money and an organized system of paper debt, public finance throughout the world was based on hard assets (gold, silver, gems, castles and the like). Now the scope of public finance is so vast that most transactions are on paper, magnetic materials, or plastic. True, a castle or other piece of real estate may be collateral for a loan, and there is a huge and measurable amount of hard assets in the world. I recently saw some data which indicates that assets in the world are about four times gross world product. That ratio varies from year to year, particularly if there is a "bubble" in real estate, stocks, or some other class of assets. But it makes sense to understand that the world's annual output of goods and services requires the build up of significant assets like machinery, transportation systems and buildings. And it's no surprise that this annual world output is valued at only about a quarter of what it cost to build the structure which permits the output.

Generally, in the world of personal finance, credit is extended to individuals and organizations on the basis of their expected ability to re-pay at a later date. This is common sense, an instinct as old as humanity. In the world of governments, however, the ability of a regime to create money and credit out of supposed thin air is very real, and is a skill practiced with great subtlety. Forgetting about metal coinage for the moment, because it is not a big factor, let us turn to paper money. In all cases, national money represents in the hands of the holder, a promise by the issuing government to redeem that money in some other paper instrument. For example, the U.S. government promises in effect to exchange a $100 bill for five $20 bills, at par without subtraction. On a larger scale, the government is willing to sell you a debt instrument, also described in dollars but re-payable in the future, in exchange for your current money.

Each dollar issuance (and the same line of thought applies to the issuance of any nation's currency), implies the promise to exchange or redeem that currency. A well-organized country can tell you just how many dollars, pounds, pesos or whatever, are issued and outstanding. But the decision of how many dollars to print, on a day-to-day basis is an arbitrary and specialized function of treasury officials, working with banking authorities. I am not being critical in saying this. In general, the world-wide availability of paper currency is good, and the failure of banks to be able to deliver it to depositors (which used to be a big problem), is now rare. However, there is always the question of "How did the money get into circulation in the first place?" The usual sources would be quoted: salaries, interest, trades, loans, etc. But supposing . . . that the Mexican government voted to *give from its treasury* 100,000 pesos to each and every Mexican citizen, and commanded its department of printing to forthwith print and distribute this paper. Would this be a good idea? What would people do with the money? Would the new money be regarded equally well with the former money still in circulation?

The ability of governments to create money, simplistically as in the Mexican example, or by other more sophisticated devices, is now endless. It is partly governed by psychological perceptions. Big and powerful nations like the U.S. have a lot of flexibility. Small nations, particularly those who have borrowed money which needs to be re-paid in a currency other than their own, have less flexibility. If Mexicans, for example, lost faith in the ability of their peso to buy anything, and at the same time were faced with paying back a big dollar loan which was taken out many years ago, the government defaults. This is basically what happened to the Russian ruble in the 1990's. And the trouble with defaults by governments is that years may go by before lenders will show any interest in loans to them.

The dilemma for governments of small and particularly of poor nations is that they find they cannot increase their internal capital without relying on outside sources for loans. Why is this? One of the main reasons is that when outside loans are granted, it is expected by all that the recipients will make a profit on the money loaned. Too often, those profits are taken out of the country and invested in hard currency countries, where the balances held are not contributing to the financial health of the small country in question. American banks are favorite repositories for such paper, sent here by people abroad who mistrust the intentions and integrity of their own governments. It is hard to legislate against this instinct on the part of perfectly honest and legitimate owners of the money. To do so would be to strike a serious blow at international capital flow and freedom of choice in business matters.

I pass over the historical question as to why God or Nature bestowed certain kinds of assets upon certain countries. This question is scarcely worthy even of a sermon or moral treatise. It is a fact that some countries have diamonds, some have gold. Others have gas and oil. Others have hydroelectric power or an inventive populace. There is scarcely a country which does not have some special asset, even if it is an invented one like being called "a nation of shop-keepers". But I believe that the building up of capital in countries which have the least of it is the most important economic problem requiring solution in the 21st century. Much hinges on it.

I have mentioned that there are only three ways for governments to acquire capital (conquest, taxation, or borrowing). Since conquest is pretty much a thing of the past, and taxation is a political matter with highly particular details for each nation, I want to discuss borrowing in its world-wide sense. There is a tremendous need for it, and indeed on the side of those who possess the resources, a tremendous need to lend the money to responsible borrowers. This mutual need has always existed, but is diluted by the populist caricature of the grasping banker and the starving debtor.

I have pointed out that the International Monetary Fund assists countries with currency problems requiring short-term loans. This specialized side of world-wide borrowing has a general high approval factor. Unless ill-informed protesters who want to restrict globalist tendencies were to bring it down, it should continue to do its job quietly and effectively as long as interrelated national currencies exist around the globe.

Another source of international borrowing is the World Bank, also an affiliate of the United Nations, whose capital is contributed by member nations. This bank is not very big in global terms, compared with the huge assets of private and national government-controlled banks. The World Bank exists to fund long-term development projects in capital-short nations. It receives more than its share of both approval and criticism. Practically all of its loans are at the behest of governments, and therefore subject to more pure political pressure than private business loans. The bank is small in world terms and it has a limited effect on the total availability of loan capital. The fact that the nations and businesses of the world have never assigned it much capital illustrates the reality that private and/or national-controlled capital is still by far the biggest factor in international capital flows.

Governments with big national budgets have the largest theoretical ability to fund big loans directly to smaller, poorer nations. Depending on your political point of view, you could accuse these bigger nations (G-7 countries and the like), of being overly tight or overly generous in their loans. The United States is not particularly generous, but on the other hand, many of the loans are dollar-denominated. This means that the United States, as the issuer of dollars, in its position as a major reserve banker for the world, is ultimately the deep-pocket behind many loans. The purchasing power of the U.S. dollar, long-range, is very powerful, whether you are a borrower or a lender.

The position of private banks like Citibank, with respect to loans made directly to smaller, poorer nations, is analogous to the position of all banks toward smaller, poorer individuals and organizations. The man in the street is right when he observes that those who need money the most have the toughest time getting it. Private banks in every country, whether big or small, exist to make money, and their governments invariably restrict their ability to make risky loans. Unless the U.S. government is prepared to subsidize transactions in some way, private banks are not going to be big volume lenders in speculative markets.

There are differences of opinion among economists about whether the world will face major price inflation or deflation in coming years. No one can say for sure, but one's judgment about this has a big effect on the availability of capital. This is not just a question of politics. No sensible lender will provide capital to a borrower if the lender thinks the borrower will pay him back in a depreciated currency.

In the name of international stability, much effort has been expended in recent times to restrain inflation and keep currency exchange rates from swinging violently. This governmental management has been attempted on a world-wide basis only recently. Economists' ability to measure the national output, trade, treasury balances, and indebtedness of nations permit such control and financial management to be dreamed about with hopes of success. I am surprised that financial leaders have succeeded as well as they have. The mechanisms for evading international panics, and leveling out purely financial difficulties among nations, have been tuned to a fine degree, with great benefits to the multitude. At the moment, short of a complete disintegration of the world's economies, I can only see the system growing in sophistication.

There is considerable discussion about the build-up of monetary reserves in surging economies like China, or even large economies which surged in the recent past, like Japan or Arabia. It turns out that these economies, with strong international export positions for which they have been paid in dollars, have taken a large number of those dollars and bought U.S. Treasury Dollar-denominated bonds. Some alarmists worry in public that a simultaneous move by these unidentified national treasuries to sell the bonds could seriously depress and deflate the whole world's financial values. I admit that there is a theoretical justification for this fear, and I recommend that the United States government continue cautious and conservative policies about dollar valuation to avoid letting it be thought that the dollar is losing purchasing power at a greater rate than other currencies.

However, history specifies at the moment that the U.S. Dollar is so predominant in world affairs that if it didn't exist you would have to invent it. In fact, it is the world's currency already, without the name to go with the title. In this respect, history has also left its calling card on the English language. Nice as it might sound for everyone in the world to learn an Esperanto which would supplant all the other languages for inter-communication, it is not going to happen at this time.

HEALTH & EDUCATION

The United States government recognized that education and health-care have much community of interest, and formed Cabinet-level agencies to deal with these matters. Since these topics have to do with everyone's personal bodily and mental well-being, one would think that they were priority items for governmental attention. However, our citizens in the U.S. are inclined to view health and education as highly individualistic and localized topics. This is changing to a more socialized, group-oriented opinion, but the change is slow, and has been unable to sustain a properly funded universal health plan. Defense, which used to go under the more honest title of "War" obviously has the preeminent position in terms of expenditure and prestige. Commercial considerations have long had a leading role in our government's thinking. Therefore, Labor, Agriculture, Commerce, and Interior have traditionally been closely interrelated with the industries of the country. However, the idea of the nation dealing with questions of individual social well-being was long regarded with suspicion; the constitution and regional habits seemed to prefer that such matters be handled by state and local governments.

Other nations have different outlooks on education, particularly, often with centralized direction in curricula and national purpose. In the U.S., the panoply of public and private secondary schools is under the direction of the states, with the federal government playing a reserve guidance position. There is a huge, diverse system of universities, not under the direction of the national government.

The Social Security System, by contrast, is a federally-conceived effort permitting forced savings plus investment returns to provide a basic stipend to retirees, but there has been no agreement on a nationally-controlled medical service plan, and politicians have broken their political swords in attempting to establish one. An interesting example giving flesh to this view of American medicine occurred when British doctors proposed the creation of a "polypill" which would be prescribed routinely for people over 55. This pill, (not yet designed in detail), would contain aspirin, cholesterol-lowering drugs, blood pressure drugs, and folic acid. The proposers of this project reason that if all citizens of this age group routinely took such a pill, an additional 11 to 12 years of life would result. Newspaper reporters asked experts for their reaction to this idea, which essentially was group medicine, providing broad public health measures based on statistical analysis. It is lowest-common-denominator medicine, analogous to fixing the emissions content of electric power plants to a certain value of "parts per million" for waste products from the smokestack. Some experts were enthusiastic about the concept, often from the practical point of view that a standard low-cost medicine, easy to take and use daily—something like toothpaste—would be of immense value to society. Others thought that Americans would never give up the notion that each one of us is entitled to the absolute best and particular treatment for our own troubles . . . and hang the cost. One Harvard professor, who said the concept had value, observed: "We're going broke with all the diagnostic tools and individual medicines. This may fit for a large number of people."

Public and private health are leading topics among all the matters one could discuss about the world's future. Any discussion which omits this, whether a political platform or candid private advice, is missing a major subject. Statistics indicate that longevity is increasing everywhere. Populations are growing. People are moving to different occupations and locations.

Under the rubric of "public health", I include sanitation, waste handling, communicable disease control, and other imposed group controls which have the effect of forcing desirable health practices even on indifferent or sometimes hostile populations. This generation's increasingly effective campaign against smoking, for example, is definitely a public health initiative.

The United States has been wrestling politically with health issues, mainly related to "who is going to pay for it?" Most of the figures I see indicate that on average, we spend about 15% of our incomes for health care, and as observers have watched this percentage rise in the last generation, there has been much wringing of hands over this alleged terrible drain on the nation's resources. I see the matter differently, feeling that the maintenance of health is such an important part of life for everyone, that the expenditures could still rise even more sharply, and be quite tolerable.

There are interesting technological twists to this economic argument, and I am surprised that there is not more commentary. Most of the arguments are based on the notion that medical care is very expensive because it requires the personal attention of high-capability professionals who command high salaries because of their scarcity. Historically this is probably true. But looking at the future, I see a variety of factors which may limit medical costs anyway, and provide more cures, longer lives, and less trauma per dollar than what we have been accustomed to.

Our first line of investigation is the cost of medications. Historically, international developers and suppliers of these things argued that high prices were necessary to provide the capital for funding even more efficacious products. It was said that the generous profit margins and high overheads of the drug companies were necessary to attract both money and talent. The world's patent laws, too, were and are invoked to support what is, in effect, a quasi-monopoly administered by a handful of major drug suppliers worldwide, like Merck or GlaxoSmithKline.

This argument is reminiscent of ideas advanced by the defenders of AT & T in the telecommunications business and of IBM in the computer business. The breakup of monopolies is always painful to monopolists, but I believe the drug business, and the public it serves, needs more sharp competition. If there were competitive manufacture of commodity drugs, the selling price of these products would decrease substantially. It is almost impossible to prove this point based on outside study of drug company financial records. Nonetheless, I believe there is a solid case to be made for increasing volumes of drug sales with steadily lowering unit costs, and greater usage penetration where the drugs are most needed.

The cost of professional care-givers like doctors and nurses can be expected to rise at a rate greater than that of the social average. Like professional educators, health care professionals need giant amounts of training, and the number of their working service years is correspondingly limited.

All of this descriptive talk about the place of high skill persons in a world that is largely peopled by unskilled persons gives way to a consideration of how the world will develop in terms of skills. Will it all happen automatically within a few years? Or will it happen by plan? Or will it *not* happen, leaving the primitive ways of ordinary folks prevailing over the structures and conceits of the highly-trained?

The development of skills in society is a sporadic wish in most parts of the world, even including the United States and other advanced economies. We hear of advances in education in lesser-developed nations like India, but the messenger who brings the news also mentions that it is hard for many to get meaningful employment in their specialty. We know now that an oversupply of personnel exists in Saudi Arabia, and that its government has discouraged and sent back to their homelands many skill-qualified people.

Various techniques, often financial in nature involving subsidies, are used as a result of governmental or private priorities for skill sets, but the overall picture is hit-or-miss. A surplus of physicists one decade . . . a shortage the next. And the same for many other specialties, ranging from farmers to secondary school teachers. I cannot worry about this, because I cannot conceive of a central authority which would have the brains or ability to make such personnel plans. No, the present allocations, accidental though they may be, are a sufficient answer to the problems posed by eternally fluid working conditions. However, the concentration of education from the start to maturity can be universal in character. That is, the core curriculum of students everywhere is and should be roughly the same for young people up to 21, the reasonable threshold of maturity. Vocational specialization comes later, and the student can vary that specialization, with society's full approval and support, according to tangible needs of the individual and society.

The biggest commercial trend in the past two centuries has been the abandonment of sustenance agriculture by populations all over the globe. The agriculture world, in synchronism with trends in other fields, has become specialized because of universal evaluation of soils, climates, markets, and the availability of capital and labor. Earlier in the book I mention the 200-year migration of the sheep industry to Australia where untrammeled land enabled monstrous herds, and new refrigeration methods made it possible for the Australians to supply meat for the whole world by ship.

There is concern that rising incomes for persons of advanced skill leave the unskilled at a relative disadvantage. There are too many of the latter, so it is said, and I have heard discussions among the well-off dismissing the poor for their insouciant, improvident behavior. Those who like to give a learned air to their distaste for the poor often speak of the need for birth control, and approve of the view ascribed to Malthus that the growth of population will surpass the world's productive ability. I reject that view, adopting the visual evidence that there are far more tasks in this world requiring labor than what is available to do the job. Specifically in the United States, labor has been in short supply for the total time in which there has been an organized picture here.

Production of food, clothing and housing has largely been mechanized throughout the world. Mass production of hard goods is universal and cheap. Communication and transportation costs are routine, and subject to vigorous cost improvements. By contrast, the care of human minds and bodies is very expensive. Education and health require one-on-one personal attention and service, with minimal opportunity for mechanization and standardization. Yet I would be happy if the defense (war) budget of the United States and all other nations were radically cut, and the money diverted to educational and health requirements.

I am particularly interested in advancing education which traverses national borders, because it is in that zone that innovation and incentive for improvement is most lacking. Happily, there has been progress during my life, but much remains to be done. Student exchanges are a universal possibility, even for modestly financed families. They were not done 100 years ago. Significant numbers of students come to the United States for university-level work, partially supported by the accidental but useful adoption of English as a lingua franca for the world. There is less movement, but great possibilities, for students in all nations to study in universities of many other nations; the greatest barrier is that nations are protective of this vital mental investment, and they don't have much excess financial or physical capacity to take on students from abroad for serious study. I know this is the case in the rich United States, where there are few scholarship supports for foreign students, either at public or private universities. Most of the serious players to whom I have talked in the U.S. are delighted to have foreign students attend their schools if they pay the full bill, and what that means is that the preponderance of such students come from families abroad who are comparatively wealthy. I have no objection to this at this moment; society is organized that way at present. Nonetheless, all nations should want to make serious allocation of resources to the education of interested foreign students.

Our six children received excellent basic education at public schools until they were ready for university experience. Then they had excellent private education at prestigious 4-year colleges, and some pursued advanced degrees. My conclusion as a parent is that practically all children should experience a university. I have observed my children's progress through life, and those of many of their age group who I have come to know. Generalizing, I will say that in the United States there is a fine college education available to whoever wants it, at the most obscure places: community colleges, state university branches, night schools, religious and technical colleges. You do *not* have to attend an Ivy League college either to be happy or successful in life.

In addition to endorsing trans-border educational experience, I am particularly interested in the theory and practice of language training. One of my greatest regrets is that I did not invest more time in serious work in foreign languages. Now I see that each person who is instrumental in international commerce, government, and educational affairs must be skilled in at least one additional language beyond his or her native tongue. In a recent trip to Japan, I visited a vocational immersion English language training school. The school caters to Japanese nationals who want to hone their English prior to expected opportunities for work and travel in the U.S. Their training is classic immersion: students are required to use only English in their classes and in off-hours from study.

The concept of total immersion language training was not new for me; it first came to my attention in an amateur vein when I was a child, and learned that my sisters, and my soon-to-be wife were enrolled at a summer camp in Vermont called Ecole Champlain. This organization required that its young clients speak only French during their entire two months of summer residence. Though that was many years ago, my wife has benefited greatly by this exposure, and retains a working knowledge of French.

I think most teaching organizations are convinced that total immersion is highly desirable. The question raised by my new acquaintances in Japan is where and under what conditions the immersion takes place. Most Japanese who come to the States operate on the idea that they will "pick up" English during their period of working in the language at sites in the U.S. I saw a contrary opinion at work, which was that the students should be drilled in English while still living in Japan, under controlled conditions. It has been found that most Japanese congregate with their peers in living circumstances when abroad, and are often working with other Japanese-speaking persons. The result is that their English exposure is far weaker than originally imagined. These observers feel that students do much better if they arrive in the States already fluent and ready to build on that strength. My instinct tells me that this is correct thinking, in preparing a student to enter any foreign language zone in a serious manner.

Another educational advantage which I feel should be more widely practiced, throughout the world, is that of basic science. The earth is increasingly dependent on technology, which gets slender attention at all levels of formal education. Understanding of the findings of physics, chemistry, and biology, for all parts of the population, would do much to improve the participation of citizens in the real world. I do not have any easy formula for doing this, because I recognize that the pool of qualified teachers is always small, and the amount of toil required is always great.

STRATEGY

It took a long time for me to figure out the difference between tactics and strategy. I used the words interchangeably when I was young. Even when I was in the Army and studying war professionally, I had a hard time distinguishing between them. Now the passage of time has made me more sensitive to the longness of strategy compared to the shortness of tactics. I employ the word "strategy" to comprise the building of dreams, the instinct of learning and advancement, and the naïve hope for the future which is the birthright of the young. Tactics is the daily contest to live.

Whether fortunately or not, I cannot say, but it happened in my life experience that by age 45 I had completed a career in business in such a way that I had an excess of assets over liabilities, and some time on my hands. This was not mid-life crisis as popularly defined, but a definite pause. At that time, it seemed to me that a large number of acquaintances, both new and old, had developed pauses in their own lives which caused them to want to talk about the future. I was in a position to listen, and spent many hours doing that: often offering advice, occasionally investing money, but in the end learning more than I taught. It was a time in American business when "entrepreneurship" came into fashion, and even in our conservative backwater, there were lots of projects . . . and risks to be taken.

In addition to refining some of my notions about business, it was also a time to re-examine many of life's other aspects. I was in a continuous state of defining and refining my own true self, testing the theories of youth against the actuality of existence.

I see now, 20 or 30 years later, how difficult it was for me . . . almost impossible . . . to change my life strategy. It was largely foretold, and had been in execution for 45 years. There were a few weak stabs at making major changes, but I went back to old patterns most of the time. (And my experience is that most of the people I sat with on my front porch . . . after all the talking was done . . . went back to doing things the way they had before.)

In my case, the happiness of my adolescence, and a mostly uneventful life through College had bestowed an optimism of spirit which was only a little diminished by the need to detour into the Army and go off to the Korean War. I had a romantic notion of marriage, and a suitable candidate was at hand, who was willing to experiment with my strategy, so by age 30 we lived a happy, modest, well-connected life. After first rejecting the notion of going into the family manufacturing business, I actually had done just that, and was starting to enjoy it. I didn't know it, but the option of developing a new strategy was already rapidly receding. Six children appeared in rapid succession, and our life seemed to be flowering.

I didn't know it then as well as I know it now: troubles inevitably occur in happy families, as well as in unhappy families. I took my own route to escape difficult personal and business problems which persisted for many years; they were not all handled successfully, and I learned the sober lesson that my great optimism about life was not capable of producing happiness and solutions for everyone. I did the best I could. In several situations it was not enough.

Since this is not a biography, I mention this intimate detail only to underscore the factor of fate and inevitability as it affected my life. Cosmic interferences ranging from love to death to war made their bids to upset the prognosis for my life . . . but basically never changed its trajectory. My life and the lives of those close to me have been mostly controlled by major trends in the world far out-weighing the personal details which have come along.

That life up until now has been one of privilege, and I doff my hat to that category, and understand it in the lives of others. Yes, there is a privileged class in the United States. It is large and also pervasive. You can find it in small towns, in medium-sized cities, in huge metropolises. The class tends to have newer members in the big, competitive cities, whereas in the smaller places it is usually the well-to-do old timers. Many, if not most of these folks are the nicest people you will ever meet. Often, they are generous. They are well-organized, and are leaders in benevolent works. They are assiduous in handing down their financial assets to descendents; their non-financial assets, such as education or religious preferences, are even more zealously nurtured.

Into such a class of people I was born, innocently enough, and raised tenderly. I do not know whether my father or mother harbored any strategy for my life. They had plenty of children, so it was not necessary to focus on me for genetic survival reasons. Since I had been warned, as mentioned earlier in the book, about the excesses of wealth, I was not surprised that there was no excess of luxury in *our* little corner of the universe. We were merely "comfortable". Again, I refer to this personal point without expanding on it. I merely identify a point of view which had an influence in the development of my own strategy for life . . . and it was handed down from above.

The course of global change started to upset the balance of our family life even as I was brought into this world in 1929. It was, in retrospect, a fateful year, but few foresaw the immense change which would occur in the next ¾ of a century, to the present point. The elite class into which I was born had started to lose their bearings and control during the first World War; the Depression starting in 1929 emphasized this decline, and World War II finished it. True, there was lots of prosperity still to come, and lots of genuine progress, but the relationship of the classes had changed forever.

We as a family possessed a substantial manufacturing business. There were dozens of such in Philadelphia, as in all American cities, and their family leaders were dukes and princes of society. I'm not sure who the kings and queens were. One would be tempted to say it was governors or presidents, but that was not the case. The world of government for my parents' generation was "the other", the dark side.

I took a different and favorable view of government from my youth, enamored by its possibilities in the United States, though ignorant of its vagaries in other places. Nonetheless, I approved of the growing consolidation of national control of the crucial factors in the country's life: health and safety, civil rights, fair commerce, etc. Then, 50 years ago, I plunged enthusiastically into the movement for *world* government: the ultimate dream, some say fantasy, of humanity. After this brief fling, the occurrence of the Korean War, and then the Cold War, plus myriad domestic preoccupations, diverted my eyes. The key thing is that I believed in the efficacy of government generally—not just for the United States, but for the entire world.

In a career in a professional commercial business, and an amateur career in politics, I encountered the best and the worst of both worlds. I escaped from financial and political traps with mind and body intact, and a view which is still optimistic. Since I have not yet reached 100, I avoid the temptation to respond to the reporter's inquiry: "Mr. Scott, to what factors do you attribute your longevity?" Nor do I have particular advice for those friends and family who might survive me. If there is anything I have concluded, it is that there are many schemes in life, and most of them will work, if intelligently pursued. A "scheme" is regarded in some parts of the English-speaking world as a devious word indicating an intent to defraud, but for American me, it is equivalent to the word "strategy".

I would like to set aside the ethical and moral part of life strategy. Virtually all people I have encountered believe they are doing the best thing for themselves, and there is no graver insult than an accusation or hint that a person is a liar. And yet we could picture the world, particularly after reading the average morning paper, as a gigantic SNAFU. It would appear that the good personal intentions of billions of people are of no effect. If we save money, we are wiped out by war or taxation. If we are kind to deer, we find the animals eating us out of house and home. If we start a business, we find that most businesses fail, and so do we. If we love, we are not loved in return. And so forth.

Recently Mary Liz and I spent a night in a Bed-and-Breakfast in Lethbridge, Alberta. At breakfast, I asked the proprietress: "What is current local thinking about the economic and political situation in Canada and the world?" (This was mostly to wake us from sleep.) "Ah," she exclaimed, "For us Mormons everything that has happened, is happening, and will happen in future is written down already. Therefore, it is not useful to indulge in such speculation." I withdrew from further discussion along this line, with the thought that a large slice of humanity believes in effect, as my friend averred, that there is nothing novel in the world. I resolved again to change the world's direction, but by what strategy?

Could it be that the explanation of my Mormon hostess is poetically, if not literally true? At first, such a suggestion is devastating to a 21st century activist who spends hours arguing and working for good causes ranging from politics to religion to commerce to art. Looking more deeply, I conclude that each of us has a need and an obligation, to live a personal life which is productive and affirmative. Each of us has a strategy for achieving the desired results. But . . . whether or not we perform well, the world considered as a total civilization is developing in a certain direction which could be described as inevitable.

A man I met recently urged on me the thought that all the cosmos is now understandable to the intelligent amateur. He must have judged me such an amateur on first introduction, and flatteringly gave me a list of books to read. Without skipping a beat or consulting his list, I made a mental note that every new scientific journal I receive contains details of staggering inconsistencies and new findings about the universe; my well-schooled wife observes that physicists have five times in her lifetime announced that they reviewed their opinions and now understand the principles of physics. So how can I argue that matters are developing in an inevitable manner? If the cosmos is unfathomable, volatile and unpredictable, how can I sense a trend, even for our little world and solar system?

Notwithstanding the fact that physicists frequently revise theory and practice about the universe, there is a well-known, consistent vision of its creation and subsequent history. This vision is sufficiently developed that we may risk general observations about it. The vision permits and even requires global understanding by all humanity. Failure to understand these matters could be fatal in one of two ways: either destruction of the world by its own hand, or such severe degradation of life on the planet as to reduce us to savage behavior or a return to pre-historic conditions. I rule out natural phenomena such as meteor hits or other apocalyptic disasters. They are entertaining to discuss, and will ultimately happen, but for ordinary civilized discourse about the next few hundred years, my assumption is that the earth will continue to spin on its axis with a biosphere capable of supporting "several" billions of human beings.

In 1982, John Naisbitt wrote *Megatrends*. His book was a leading work in visualizing the future through American eyes. Its sub-heading was: "Ten new directions transforming our lives". Much of what he had to say is pertinent and is related to economics, politics, and demographics. He was prescient in his predictions of the information technology industry, of the change in global trading conditions, and numerous other topics. My aim in this work is to expand that vision to a world basis, and to show that there is little mystery about how the organizational portion of the world's work will be accomplished. In addition, since man does not live by bread alone, I offer opinions about personal and private endeavors. There is more room for surprises in those topics than there is about commerce and government, but that they are subject to "megatrends" I have little doubt.

In other parts of this book, I infer many opinions and attitudes toward the social process, involving group activities, such as those exercised by companies, churches, governments, or similar entities. There is another aspect of this as it pertains to strategy. It seems that humankind is dealing with biological connections which generally go under the heading of "family", and most of us study our peers and remark that Suzy is 'like' Aunt Sally, or John 'resembles' cousin Nicholas. We like those comparisons, and they offer a practical tip as to the development of evolution. Often in quiet moments we ponder the traits of each up-coming generation, wondering whether certain types of thought, action and appearance will be maintained in future or not.

My aim is always to describe the past as accurately as possible, when asked, but not to advise people too heavily about specific courses of action. Our people on both sides of the house, (my wife and all of our known ancestors for several generations), were almost universally members of the responsible middle class. They were inventors, clergymen, farmers, rent collectors, housewives, soldiers . . . altogether the glue of the much-praised middle class which supposedly is the foundation of our European/North American civilization. On the whole they were not artists, aristocrats, or celebrities. You won't find them in history books. They were Bible-quoting, particularly in the Scott and Furst lines. They were heavily engaged in orthodox Christianity as a guide to everyday life. On the whole, they created more assets than they needed to live, with the result that their descendants live comfortably, without apparent strain. Is it desirable to continue this trend? Do we have any choice?

The desire to protect and control the lives of younger affiliates is nearly universal, and the concept of the inviolable "will" or "last words" or "tradition" of the forebears is still powerful. It haunts the psyche of great nations as well as families; we daily see the efforts of the powerful to reinforce the notion that a particular nation or clan is favored or blessed by the power of the universe. This makes for exciting theater, but in the real world I see the exercise of cooperation and the making of deals. In fact, a more-or-less universal set of values, both private and public, is leveling the world scene. Many of the quirks of religion, class, and occupation are thinning out. Americans are sometimes criticized as being mindless TV viewers with a standardized non-value system, and shortly this criticism will be leveled at the whole world . . . with some justice.

Alarmist feeling exists in some circles that the world is about to be devoured by a bunch of fanatics, and that our adoption of a triumphalist military strategy can allow the decent, civilized world to protect itself from devilish social developments. I see it differently, and I argue that the amazing interchange of human opinion which has saturated the known world offers the opportunity for settlement of most of the world's perplexities without the horrors of general war or national hatred. I don't know which hazards are worse for the world, biological, atomic or psychological murder, but I feel that the vast majority of humankind wants stability, will vote for it, and ultimately will find it. Birth and death we cannot at present avoid, but the solutions to social problems are there for us to see.

I have tried for 60 years to integrate the sensible aspects of my own life strategy (essentially trying to lead a happy and productive existence . . . the natural objective of most people), with a larger strategy to improve the world. I can't help it. It comes with the territory. Call it hubris, call it noblesse oblige, call it religious fanaticism. The fact is I was always conscious of a desire to see things better . . . always a creature of hope for the future and a will to help. This was the guiding spirit of the American population, too, for which I take no credit or blame. However, I use it as the excuse to offer this book, and to examine strategy among other items.

FORWARD THOUGHTS

After investigating communism, religion, socialism, capitalism, internationalism, and other road maps for humanity, I built a life among the capitalists of this world. I thought that the work of government would interplay with the world of capital to produce optimum results for all. I simplified my analysis by setting aside the concerns of religion and of class and gender, admitting all the while that from those three alone much mischief could originate. I reasoned that the power to direct the day-by-day concerns of people in their economic life was the most important equation which was almost solved. If the world's government and commerce (largely intertwined then and intertwined now) could be put in balance, then, said I to myself, I could feel justified at the end of life if I had contributed something to it.

Political parties were an attractive force. It was obvious to the neophyte that they were avenues for personal advancement; to the naïve, it was plausible that they had to do with "issues". As I advanced in political activism, I found what every mature politician has discovered through the ages: individual opinion and personality counted more than pure issues. As I studied Roosevelt's New Deal, and came to understand the huge compromises which were necessary to advance the "issues" of the Democratic Party as it then existed, I came to a high respect for any party in a huge diversified country which attempts to market itself as a force to be elected and given the magisterial power of the nation. In later years, I had to stand away from traditional party politics because I could no longer in conscience say in public that my party was right and the other was wrong.

I followed a similar analysis in the formal business world where I made the cash living that permitted me and my family to enjoy the usual rewards of comfortable modern life. I saw the vast compromises needed for a far-flung business to exist successfully. Where a small family business became hundreds of employees, and then thousands, the complexities demanded compromise along the exact same lines suggested by political life. Poor divisions vs. rich divisions; princes of the corporate suite vs. labor; technicians vs. administrators. And so forth. Today, when I observe a new corporate chieftain in a TV interview or ringing the opening bell on the New York Stock Exchange, I listen doubtfully to the program advanced. I know that until men or women have lived the life and walked the walk of compromise, they are amateurs until proven by fire and sword. I never was successful in seizing the top job of a big organization, possibly because I could never bring myself to give it unending, unflagging adherence and belief, and to indulge in necessary compromises behind the scenes.

However, I am very much of a facilitator, trying to induce others to take positions which will advance my own ideas. Through the years I have thrown into life's kettle a thousand ideas at no charge, with the hope that others will take them up and make them into reality.

Such thoughts prevail when I think of the organization of the whole of humanity, once contemplated as a world government and/or the triumph of world capitalism. I have moved beyond parties and beyond the organized structures of both government and private enterprise. This is not to say that these edifices will cease. It is more an assertion that there are ways for outsiders like myself to help move these organisms in right directions.

Since the second Gulf War in Iraq, there have been discouraged feelings in many countries about the ability of the United Nations to be a coordinating force for the world. These feelings have been particularly intense among those who did not favor the unilateral military action of the United States in invading Iraq without full sanction of the UN Security Council. If the U.S. is indeed the richest and militarily most powerful nation in the world, and it snubs the UN, then what hope is there for action? There is divided opinion now in the U.S. within the two political parties on international matters. Almost no theoretical discussion about foreign policy occurs, and civic energy in the field is lacking.

Working with other political forces which have compatible, already-developed world-wide positions is an attractive thought. Probably the most successful ideology with a strong foothold in most countries is the ecological/conservationist movement. The second most widely-held ideology is that of the business class. This should by no means be ignored. It is probably true that the development of global organizations has not been broadly supported by business, except on an ad hoc basis. Nonetheless, as businesses and their owners have increasingly become internationalists, a measurable bias has occurred in favor of measures which are seen as promoting stability, security of property rights, and other matters of serious interest to the world's business class. A third gigantic constituency is the religious community of all faiths. Their interests are parallel to the moral and philosophical objectives I am talking about, although for reasons I explain in other parts of the book, I do not see them taking the lead.

A fourth constituency which has its main existence in the U.S., and therefore cannot be regarded as universal, is the continued influence of private capital aimed at secular enthusiasms. We call such set-asides "foundations", and they are a peculiarly rich and western way of financing good works. It is not possible to generalize about their purposes, which cover every enthusiasm of humankind. However, much of the money supports community programs such as art museums, symphony orchestras, and hospitals. A few of the bigger pots of assets support international development (e.g., Ford Foundation). Some favor higher education; a few like Pew Charitable Trusts work at innovative social programs. Except for the biggest foundations which have diversified and taken on a public political role, most of the smaller ones continue their unabated interest in the project favored by the initiator.

It is difficult to foresee that foundations—essentially the preserve of a handful of wealthy individuals seeking to preserve their name or purposes into perpetuity—can have impact in coalescing mutual interests around the globe. They are very useful for particular purposes. Many applaud when they succeed in particular projects, and their sons and daughters are pleased to receive some grant or stipend which assists them to be journalists or artists. Or perhaps a town in East Africa receives a new water system. In general, though, the resources of foundations are limited, and it is difficult to persuade the public to donate money to them.

There may be other natural constituencies which will arise in future, as one thinks about possible strategies. For example, the "workers of the world" exalted by Marx, turned out not to have a constituency in both the first and second world wars, or since. It appears that the fragmentation of labor, and its diminished prestige in comparison with capital, rules against this as a fruitful field. But that could change, and such constituencies as Arts, Sports, Education, and Entertainment probably have more potential for human interchange. I have pointed out in other parts of this work that the imprimatur of celebrities is more profound than that of politicians.

Thus, without predicting a course of action, my view at present is that attempting to secure improved global structures will come not through the publication of tracts and discussion of laws and by-laws, but probably through practical arrangements which evolve through non-traditional channels. To put it simplistically, a program by the basketball industry to have a world-wide league would require universally-accepted vocabulary, uniform statistics, global rules of the game. The confidence which could be built among the world's ordinary folks by such a program would be truly suggestive of what is possible in more traditional governmental concerns like migration, citizenship, taxation, and other supposedly sophisticated matters.

I have a feeling that while the great traditional power bases of the world oscillate, we and our immediate progeny will witness a more organized, more peaceful existence, with a higher level of personal accomplishment for all. No, that is not one of my daytime dreams. It is simply that humanity is approaching maturity, and I am the ultimate optimist.

Printed in the United States
24167LVS00001B/325